W9-BBO-607

YOUNG PEOPLE AND SOCIETY

Young People and Society

82599

TED TAPPER

LIBRARY

ARCHON BOOKS

1972

First published in 1971
by Faber and Faber Limited
3 Queen Square London WC1
First published in the United States of America by
Archon Books
The Shoe String Press, Inc.
995 Sherman Avenue, Hamden
Connecticut, 06514
Printed in Great Britain

ISBN 0–208–01249–4 All rights reserved

© *Ted Tapper 1971*

C
2OL
GT
T3
1971a

To
LYNN AND CLIVE

PREFACE

In recent years there has been an enormous expansion of research work in the field of socialization. This has affected a number of disciplines within the social sciences: sociology, social psychology and political science. This book is a part of that expanding interest. It examines how young people differ in their attitudes to the world around them, and their perception of the opportunities available to them. The scope of the questions is wide, covering political and social issues. There is an analysis of the various forces which shape the adolescent's perspectives. More particularly there is an endeavour to assess the relative influence of social class and the structure of the educational system. It is hoped, therefore, that this book will have a wide appeal; proving to be of interest to a variety of social scientists as well as to those with a more strictly defined educational interest. The attention of the latter should be increased by those sections which examine the merits of comprehensive education.

Another important task is to build a model of the socialization process; a picture of how different influences come to bear upon young people in English society. It involves tracing the progress of the child from his family environment into the educational system, and finally how he is fed on to the job market. There is ample evidence to show that a very special affinity has evolved between the socio-economic structure and the educational system. In fact many educational reforms are directed at changing this relationship. It is this established connection which lies at the heart of the model.

A number of people assisted in the preparation of this book. Above all I must thank Professor Richard Rose and Dr. A. H. Halsey; as well as being a constant source of ideas, any fluency in style that the

PREFACE

book may possess owes much to their endeavours. Both the University of Manchester and Enfield College of Technology provided financial assistance which greatly facilitated the completion of the survey and the analysis of the questionnaires. For the large sample size I owe much to certain directors of education, headmasters, teachers and of course the adolescents themselves. Dr. Gerry Dickinson, now of the University of British Columbia, provided invaluable help in construction of the statistical tests. I could not finish without a final word of thanks to Roger Moore, John Seagrave, Jeff Alterman and my wife, Lynn. Coding and checking tables and text is a tedious but very necessary task.

TED TAPPER

CONTENTS

FROM SELECTIVE TO COMPREHENSIVE EDUCATION

In the 1960s the most controversial, and perhaps the most important, changes in the English educational system took place at the secondary level. Throughout the decade there was a haphazard changeover from tripartism to the comprehensive principle. While it is not easy to define what the aims of a comprehensive school ought to be it is reasonable to suggest that they should remove the blatant defects of the highly selective tripartite system. The objectives of this first chapter are two-fold: to review briefly the body of research which illustrates the limitations of tripartism, and to discuss some of the problems that will continue to challenge, and possibly frustrate, the ideals of comprehensive education.

The inherent class bias of the selective process has been well documented. The grammar schools have been the preserve of middle class adolescents, while less prestigious forms of secondary education cater for the interests of children from working class families. As long ago as 1922 Tawney could argue, 'The organization of education on the lines of class, though qualified in the last twenty years, has characterized the English system of public education since its very inception, has been a symptom, an effect, and a cause of the control of the lives of the mass of men and woman by a privileged minority.'[1] Floud and Halsey carried out much of the pioneer research into the effects of the 1944 Education Act. They show that the percentage of working class boys gaining free places in the grammar schools has actually declined, because the Act increased the competition from middle class adolescents. Both prior to and post 1944

[1] R. H. Tawney, *Secondary Education for All*, London, Allen and Unwin, 1922, p. 33.

'the class chances' of working class children entering the grammar schools compared very unfavourably with middle class adolescents.[2]

It is not simply a question of inequitability at the point of entry into the grammar schools for there are also class differentials in the distribution of the rewards which the grammar schools have to offer. The way a pupil profits from his school career can be measured in a number of different ways: staying at school beyond the minimum school leaving age, obtaining a number of recognized certificates, and gaining entry into institutions of higher education. The Robbins Report illustrates the large class differences for some of these measures. The Report states, 'The proportion of middle class children who reach degree level courses is eight times as high as the proportion from working class homes, and even in grammar schools it is twice as high. As has been shown, the difference in grammar schools is not chiefly due to lower intelligence, but rather to early leaving. However, it is not only in these schools that the wastage of ability is higher among manual working class children. There is much evidence to show that both before the age of eleven, and in later years, the influence of environment is such that the differences in measured ability between social classes progressively widen as children grow up.'[3]

Underlying tripartism was the assumption that children had different ability levels, and that it was in the interests of all pupils that these distinctive strata should be taught separately. The allocation of the eleven-year-old school children to the various types of secondary schools has generally been determined by I.Q. tests. There are other aspects to many 11+ examinations besides the I.Q. test but it is fair to say that the attempt to assess the pupil's intelligence quotient is the most important, and certainly the most publicized, part of the selection process. The link between social class and I.Q. rests upon the claim that I.Q. is influenced by social factors, so that individuals who do well in such tests are generally speaking merely

[2] J. Floud (ed.), A. H. Halsey and F. M. Martin, *Social Class and Educational Opportunity*, London, Heinemann, 1956, p. 51.

[3] Committee on Higher Education, *The Demand for Places in Higher Education*, London, H.M.S.O., 1963, p. 46. The point is reinforced by the findings of Floud and Halsey that, 'the great improvement already noted in the proportion of working class boys remaining at school beyond the age of compulsory attendance has not resulted in a greater proportion of them completing the grammar school course in the approved way by obtaining a leaving certificate.' See *ibid.*, p. 122.

those with the better social environments. There has been considerable conflict between the adherents of this position and those who argue that I.Q. is basically an hereditary characteristic.

Vernon points out that the original motives for introducing intelligence tests were very worthy. 'Their aim was "to discount the advantages of a large school with individual attention and special coaching" and to devise "a selection procedure which gave equal, or almost equal chances to an unprepared candidate". They hoped they would go some way towards achieving their aim by using intelligence tests.'[4] Furthermore such tests provide the working class child with a better chance of a grammar school place than attainment tests or teachers' assessments. 'The abolition of standardized tests, particularly intelligence tests, and reliance on older and more conventional types of examination (e.g. essays), on school reports, and interviews, tend to increase the advantages of the middle class over the working class child.'[5]

The current feeling is that it is meaningless to pose either/or alternatives; that in fact intelligence stems from the interaction of environmental and hereditary influences. This interpretation receives strong support from Troday, '. . . unless the populations have been artificially produced by special breeding programmes designed to eliminate genetic variety, the causes of variance are always both genetic and environmental, and the variance can be partitioned into three components, genetic variance, environmental variance and variance arising from genotype-environment interaction. In other words we may classify the causes of variance into these three groups and assign them relative importance. This is true of every continuously varying character that has been adequately studied of any species of outbreeding organism. It is undoubtedly true of I.Q. variation.'[6]

Regardless of the relative merits and shortcomings of I.Q. testing,

[4] P. E. Vernon, *Secondary School Selection*, London, Methuen, 1957, pp. 23–4.
[5] P. E. Vernon, 'Development of Current Ideas about Intelligence Tests', in J. E. Meade and A. S. Parkes (eds.), *Genetic and Environmental Factors in Human Ability*, London, Oliver and Boyd, 1966, p. 3. In support of the position that intelligence is primarily an hereditary item see C. Burt, 'Ability and Income', *British Journal of Educational Psychology*, Volume 13, 1943, pp. 171–190.
[6] J. M. Troday, 'Geneticism and Environmentalism', in J. E. Meade and A. S. Parkes (eds.), *Biological Aspects of Social Problems*, London, Oliver and Boyd, 1965, p. 96.

specific objections can be made of the way it has been used for secondary school selection in England. In the first place there are doubts about the long-term predictive value of such tests. These doubts are increased when it is recognized that I.Q. is not a static entity.[7] It is unfair, therefore, to separate children at the age of eleven. This is especially true when the opportunities for retesting at later ages are hardly ever accepted. There is no universal level of performance which automatically gives the individual a grammar school place. In reality this has been decided by the number of grammar school places available in the locality. Thus the absurd position arose in which adolescents living in one community with a particular I.Q. score were excluded from grammar schools; in another community adolescents with exactly the same score were admitted to grammar schools.

In the tripartite system there are three types of secondary schools: grammar, technical and secondary modern. Only a few local authorities have established technical secondary schools and so for the most part there is a simple dual system. The majority of schools have set up streaming divisions which are commonly based upon the alleged differences in the academic ability of their pupils. There is increasing evidence that streaming acts as a self-fulfilling prophecy; individuals who have been classified as failures often live up to—or should it be down to—their reputation. On the basis of evidence obtained from teaching and research in primary schools Jackson concludes, 'There is one curious point about the social effects of streaming. "A" classes, segregated and streamlined, were an elite in training. But "C" classes, separate and inward-turning, were altogether a textbook illustration of how to create the culture of the gang.'[8] This trend is probably most pronounced in the secondary modern schools. Hargreaves looks at the creation of two very contrasting subcultures: the academic top stream and the delinquent bottom streams.[9] This is not to deny that the same social movement takes place in the grammar schools. Lacey graphically describes the impact of streaming upon incoming grammar school pupils. They have left behind them their established junior school status, and there is now a

[7] On this see Vernon, *Secondary School Selection*, p. 104.

[8] Brian Jackson, *Streaming: An Educational System in Miniature*, London, Routledge, 1964, p. 126.

[9] David H. Hargreaves, *Social Relations in a Secondary School*, London, Routledge and Kegan Paul, 1967.

competition to create new havens of security. The academic weaklings gravitate towards the bottom stream, forming an anti-school clique. While the first-year sorting out process is under way many pupils suffer from a variety of emotional problems.[10]

These objections to the selective system can be summarized in the following terms: there has been a premature, rigid defining of the levels of opportunity, harmful to both the adolescent and society; class and academic segregation hinders the development of social harmony and severely restricts the size of the pool of talent. The 1944 Education Act was supposed to establish parity of esteem between the secondary schools but clearly this has not taken place. From this failure stems most of the problems of the tripartite system. As Vernon states, 'The parity of esteem envisaged in the 1944 Education Act is unlikely to be achieved so long as the curricula, vocational opportunities and social prestige of these schools are so widely differentiated. Hence instead of "allocation by age, ability and aptitude" we are faced with highly competitive selection to the grammar schools.'[11] Taylor claims that failure to establish parity of prestige occurs because certain types of secondary schools are more likely to provide their pupils with the style of education – including those all-important GCE certificates – which leads to a secure income and a prestigious job. 'This study is an attempt to trace the effect of influences on the Modern school, illustrating, among other things the difficulties of reconciling an educational system based on premises of equality and the provision of a liberal education with the realities of occupational stratification.'[12] The secondary modern schools adjusted their educational programme to the demands of the occupational structure; they introduced a variety of leaving certificates, including the GCE examination, with the end result that a potentially highly flexible outlook grew more rigid. Taylor concludes, 'The attempt to establish a new concept of secondary education for the bulk of the population, untrammelled by the demands of the school certificate or other examinations designed chiefly for university entrance, has met with conspicuous failure.'[13]

[10] Colin Lacey, 'Some Sociological Concomitants of Academic Streaming in a Grammar School', *British Journal of Sociology*, Volume 17, 1966, pp. 245–262.
[11] P. E. Vernon, *Secondary School Selection*, p. 167.
[12] William Taylor, *The Secondary Modern School*, London, Faber, 1963, p. 14.
[13] *ibid.*, p. 160.

The Comprehensive principle

As the early quote from Tawney suggests there is a long history of dissatisfaction with the selective secondary system. Referring to the reaction to the Hadow Report and the Spens Report, which between them were primarily responsible for advocating the tripartite arrangements, Monks states, 'A considerable body of opinion, however, was against selection and separate schools, and an alternative much advocated in the 1920s by the Labour party and its supporters was the multi-lateral school.'[14] He continues, 'The elimination of selection and the provision of a wide variety of courses are notions fundamental to "comprehensive" education and it is here, in the discussions on the multi-lateral school, that the roots of the comprehensive idea may be traced.'[15] In more recent years the debate has risen to a crescendo and, as expected, the two major political parties have been on opposite sides of the fence. It is probably fair to say that the Conservative party has been more concerned at improving the selective system, including the possible abolition of the 11+, rather than discarding the principle of selection *per se*. The Labour party have definitely come out in favour of comprehensive schools but it was only after holding office for four years that the Wilson Government actually proposed introducing legislation which would impose such a system upon all local education authorities.[16]

Definitions of comprehensive education have been rather confused. By 1947 the Ministry of Education envisaged the comprehensive schools catering for all the secondary education of all the children in a given area without organizing the school into the three distinctive units of the tripartite set-up.[17] The debate in the 1950s and '60s centred around the evils of selection as opposed to the merits of a grammar school education. The Conservative party argued that the Labour party was intent on abolishing grammar schools in spite of their record of academic success. Labour party spokesmen were very

[14] T. G. Monks, *Comprehensive Education in England and Wales*, Slough, Bucks, National Foundation for Educational Research, 1968, p. 1.

[15] *ibid.*, p. 1.

[16] On February 4th, 1970, a bill compelling local authorities to submit plans for comprehensive education, was introduced to the House of Commons. The bill was not passed and Circular 10/70, subsequently introduced by the Conservative Government, gives the local authorities considerable discretion over their arrangements for secondary education.

[17] See Monks, *op. cit.*, p. 2.

sensitive to such attacks, for they realised the strong hold of the grammar school image upon many of their working class supporters. Hugh Gaitskell countered, 'Are we to confine the chance of a grammar school education to those who pass the 11+ examination and slam the door of opportunity in the face of other children? This is the Tory idea. Or shall we abolish the 11+ examination and give every child a continuing opportunity of the education–grammar or technical–for which they are best suited?'[18] This was reinforced by the Labour party's 1959 policy statement, 'We nail the lie that our aim is to abolish grammar school education. On the contrary, we shall open it up to every child who can benefit by it, and extend the tradition and standards of the grammar school throughout secondary education.'[19] In effect, therefore, the comprehensive schools were to incorporate grammar school ideals and extend them to a wider range of school children.

The early academic literature, the somewhat later governmental committees, and the more recent and wider debate, all stress the need to remove the rigid selectivity of the tripartite system. Comprehensive education is seen as the major means of achieving this objective. The Comprehensive Schools Committee puts forward the central goal in the following terms: 'We wish to see equality of opportunity in education achieved by:

1. The elimination of selection, by examinations or any other means, at the age of transfer to secondary education.
2. The end of the segregation of children in different types of secondary school, and the rejection of the idea that separate but equal types of education can or should be provided.
3. The exploration of different ways in which the comprehensive ideal may be realized.
4. The rapid introduction of comprehensive education and the provision by the Government of the necessary finance.'[20]

This line of thinking has been supported by numerous high ranking politicians. Anthony Crosland, speaking as the Secretary of State for Education, claimed that the movement towards comprehensive

[18] Hugh Gaitskell, New Year Message to the Labour Party, 31st December, 1958. Quoted in Taylor, *op. cit.*, p. 153.
[19] *The Future Labour Offers You*, issued by the Labour Party in 1959. Quoted in Taylor, *op. cit.*, p. 153.
[20] A Comprehensive Schools Committee publication of 1965.

education, '. . . represents a strong and irresistible pressure in British society to extend the rights of citizenship.'[21] In 1967 Patrick Gordon Walker, describing Government policy, said that, 'selection and segregation in secondary education are harmful to the best interests of children, and they should be brought to an end as soon as possible.'[22] The most detailed statement is found in Circular 10/65 issued in July 1965 by the Department of Education and Science. The Department was prepared to sanction a number of contrasting comprehensive schemes as well as permit local authorities to move gradually in the direction of the proposed policy through interim stages if required.[23] The optimistic phase, however, is still very evident, 'A comprehensive school aims to establish a school community in which pupils over the whole ability range and with differing interests and backgrounds can be encouraged to mix with each other, gaining stimulus from the contacts, and learning tolerance and understanding in the process.'[24] In spite of the optimism the possibilities for *de facto* segregation were recognized: 'But particular comprehensive schools will reflect the characteristics of the neighbourhood in which they are situated; if their community is less varied and fewer of the pupils come from homes which encourage educational interests, schools may lack the stimulus and vitality which schools in other areas enjoy.'[25] However, this problem can be circumvented by careful planning on the part of the local authorities, 'The Secretary of State therefore urges authorities to ensure, when determining cachment areas, *that schools are as socially and intellectually comprehensive as is practicable.*'[26]

Superficial analysis might suggest that the introduction of comprehensive education will, within itself, remove many of the forms

[21] Speech by Anthony Crosland at the North of England Education Conference, January 7th, 1966.

[22] Quoted in *The Times*, September 19th, 1967.

[23] Department of Education and Science, *The Organisation of Secondary Education* (Circular 10/65), London, H.M.S.O., 1965. The difference between the approved and interim proposals is that the latter involve some form of separation between those pupils who intend to continue their education after the compulsory school leaving age, and those who wish to leave as soon as they are legally permitted; the favoured arrangements envisage all pupils attending the same secondary schools with at least a school leaving age of 16, and transference to other secondary schools not taking place until then.

[24] *ibid.*, Section 111(v), paragraph 36.

[25] *ibid.*, Section 111(v), paragraph 36.

[26] *ibid.*, Section 111(v), paragraph 36 (emphasis added).

of selectivity. The question of the school's social bias should disappear; there is only one type of secondary school and it will include the range of social classes appropriate to its locality. As all pupils are transferred to the same type of school, in many districts all move on to the same school, then there will be no need for I.Q. testing. The comprehensive school is better equipped to deal with the late developers; pupils do not have to move from one kind of secondary school to another.

The apparent gains must be examined more closely. Is it possible that the state system of secondary education will ever be completely comprehensive? A combination of economic and political factors are working against this. At present there are numerous chances to opt out of those comprehensive schemes in existence; the intelligent adolescent, living in an area serviced by a comprehensive school, can frequently arrange to attend a grammar school in a nearby neighbourhood. In most cases the parents are only too willing to pay the extra travelling expenses. The comprehensive school is in effect creamed of many of its brightest pupils. Given the nature of the class distribution of I.Q., plus the middle class parents' high regard for the grammar school, it is mainly the middle class adolescents who are opting out of the system.[27] This pattern is prevalent in the London area where there are many grammar and comprehensive schools in close proximity.

It is also necessary to consider the particular comprehensive schemes which have been proposed. At this stage Circular 10/65 is very pertinent. All the approved proposals, except the orthodox comprehensive school with an age range of 11 to 18, establish different stages of secondary education, with separate schools for each stage. Past research suggests that, where a breaking point exists at the age of 16, the schools will tend to lose many of their working class pupils.[28] Where there is no formal division, informal barriers may

---

[27] The attachment of the middle class parent to the grammar schools is illustrated by the Middlesbrough and South West Hertfordshire study; several middle class parents were prepared to send their children to private schools if they failed the 11 +. See Floud, Halsey and Martin, *op. cit.*, p. 76. This raises the whole question of the relationship of the private schools, including the direct grant grammar schools, to the state sector.

[28] Only one of the four approved schemes has a formal breaking point at the age of 16. Wherever transfers take place at an earlier age, then working class pupils will probably be assigned in disproportionate numbers to the bottom streams in this new stage of their secondary education.

still be erected. Thus the older age groups in the comprehensive schools could be formed from a very select pupil intake.

The 1965 circular is naive about how to overcome the problems posed by the ecological make-up of the areas in which the schools are located. In the larger cities it may not always be possible to form socially heterogeneous catchment areas without causing considerable problems to the children of secondary school age. If diversity is required then adolescents may have to be transported over fairly long distances to their schools. Middle class parents could raise many objections to any plan which envisaged their own children being educated in schools situated in slum or twilight areas of the city. However if there is little chance of adolescents from different social backgrounds being able to mix throughout their school careers then this undermines one of the central claims made on behalf of the comprehensive schools—that social interaction will assist the cause of social harmony.[29]

There are certain similarities between English and American problems of segregation. In the former case the ghettoes are composed of working class families, and in the latter case of Negroes. To create a socially heterogeneous school it is necessary to overcome the obstacles posed by socially homogeneous neighbourhoods. In the United States it appears that most of the burdens of encouraging social diversity fall upon the Negroes rather than the middle class whites. In other words there are plenty of Negro children having to bus out to the suburbs but not many white children attending ghetto schools. If the English local authorities ever take the Department's plea seriously then it will be interesting to see if they also take into account the rather bitter American experiences.

One crucial obstacle to the removal of selectivity is the internal organization of the individual schools. In this respect their streaming arrangements are very important. If there is streaming then the criteria on which it is based is all-important. It is quite possible to have pupils within a comprehensive school from a wide range of

[29] The quotes from Circular 10/65 indicate the stress that has been placed upon this idea. Townsend adds, 'To these I would add a number of social arguments, which are really educational arguments in the widest sense. More children not only have access to a wide range of skills—from turning a lathe to learning Russian. They have access to a wide cross-section of children who have different cultural backgrounds, and different kinds of talent.' See Peter Townsend, 'Argument for Comprehensive Schools', *Comprehensive Education*, No. 1, 1965, p. 8.

class backgrounds, with very different levels and types of academic ability, and still ensure their almost total segregation from each other. Townsend is very aware of this problem: 'But, finally, we need to recognize that in applying the comprehensive principle to the school system we are doing no more than breaking with the past so that we can make a fresh start. We are not solving all our educational problems, only adopting a framework which will make the task easier. There are rigidly separate streams in some comprehensive schools with little movement between one stream and another. Curricular and extra-curricular activities are devised so that there is a minimum of social interaction.'[30] His enthusiasm, however, is still close to the surface: 'But at least there will be a minimum fulfilment of the principle of equality of educational opportunity and a corporate social unity which may even spill over into adult life.'[31] It is perhaps a little premature to think of 'equality of educational opportunity and a corporate social unity' until rigid streaming arrangements have first been removed. These goals cannot be achieved independently of the type of comprehensive school favoured by the local authority.

The limited amount of research on comprehensive education tentatively supports the claim that selectivity is not eliminated in the comprehensive schools but merely reappears in a new disguise. On the basis of information collected from a London comprehensive school Holly concludes, 'Streaming by ability within the comprehensive school does not seem, pace Dr. Young, to result in producing a new elite based on attainment or intelligent quotient: it seems merely to preserve the traditional class bias of educational selection.'[32] In nearly all the facets of the educational process that Holly investigated, the middle class adolescents fared far better than their working class peers. On the basis of this evidence, he feels, 'Social class seems to be a powerful variable in nearly all aspects of "profiting" from the school. Not only does it tend to dominate scholastic achievement in the sense of the "stream" structure but it is also an important factor in "late development". Those pupils—often quoted triumphantly by heads of comprehensive schools—who find themselves following advanced sixth form courses in spite of having been graded quite low in ability at 11+, tend to be drawn heavily from favourable home

[30] *ibid.*, p. 8.   [31] *ibid.*, p. 8.
[32] D. N. Holly, 'Profiting from a Comprehensive School: Class, Sex and Ability', *British Journal of Sociology*, Volume 16, 1965, p. 157.

backgrounds. Similarly, when allowance is made for sex variation in attitude, it is middle class pupils who derive most from the activities provided by the school outside the curriculum, while middle class pupils are disproportionately represented among those fifth-formers who are chosen as prefects—less a function of teacher-bias, probably, than of school-centredness on the part of these young people themselves.'[33]

Douglas's assessment is more tenuous, 'The observations (reported in this chapter) give no clear indications of the strengths and weaknesses of the comprehensive schools. They provide some evidence that even in the late 1950s these schools were fulfilling the hopes of their founders in encouraging the manual working class pupils to remain longer at school and to take the General Certificate of Education. On the other hand they also provide evidence that aspirations for further education may be dampened in the comprehensive schools.'[34] Douglas also perceives that structural change is not automatically the road to salvation: 'The fact that inequalities existed within the old selective system does not mean that they will disappear when selective examinations are abolished; and the fact that it is the pupils from poor homes who have been handicapped in the past, does not necessarily mean that they will lose these handicaps when comprehensive education becomes universal.'[35]

Streaming within the comprehensive schools can, therefore, reintroduce all the traditional aspects of segregation: the rigid separation of social classes, the apparent depressing of ability and interest, the creation of a socially alienated group of pupils, and the curtailment of aspirations and opportunities to the detriment of both the individual and the society at large. Although experiments in streaming are increasing it is true that separation, based on levels of academic ability, is still very much the norm.[36] As Vernon says, 'Nevertheless we would venture to point out, first, that no one, except perhaps a few left-wing enthusiasts, intends to eliminate ability groupings in such schools.'[37]

[33] *ibid.*, pp. 156–7.

[34] J. W. B. Douglas, J. M. Ross and H. R. Simpson, *All Our Future*, London, Peter Davies, 1968, p. 64.

[35] *ibid.*, p. 65.

[36] For example, see Ann Glennerster, 'Comprehensive Schemes Analysed', *Where*, 29, 1967, pp. 25–7. Lindsey March, 'Which are the Unstreaming Comprehensive Schools?', *Where*, 33, 1967, pp. 4–6.

[37] P. E. Vernon, *Secondary School Selection*, p. 49.

The scepticism, relating to the actual changes which comprehensive education will introduce, is increasing. Reviewing Monks's *Comprehensive Education in England and Wales*, *The Times* made the following statements, 'By those who have all along advocated comprehensive schools for reasons of social equality the conclusion has already been drawn: abolish streaming. Streamed comprehensives do not fulfil their hopes, largely because of the ineradicable influence of the home on scholastic performance. So once again, without the evidence necessary to back their judgment, they propose to press the reform a stage further by insisting that children be taught in mixed ability groups. They are unable to show that even that would correct the tendencies which offend them.'[38] The article continues, 'Instead of looking for more powers to compel local authorities to abolish all selective schools, the Government should use its influence to restrain comprehensive extremists, at least until it has the results of the research into these disputed questions which it has itself commissioned.'[39]

There are, therefore, these opposing views on the relative advantages and disadvantages of comprehensive schools. It is fair to say that there has been a general scaling down of earlier claims; the heady days of the late 1950s have passed away, probably forever. The central questions which needed to be asked are straightforward: 'What kinds of changes, if any, do the comprehensive schools introduce?', 'Why do these changes take place?' and finally, 'Who do they most affect?' These are just some of the questions which will be raised, and hopefully at least partially answered, in the following chapters.

[38] *The Times*, October 22nd, 1968, p. 3.   [39] *ibid.*, p. 3.

2

EDUCATION AND THE
SOCIALIZATION PROCESS

The failure to appreciate that education is part of a wider learning experience undermines attempts to introduce social change through educational reform. If comprehensive schools are to have different social and educational consequences from the selective system of secondary education then the part they play in the overall learning experience must also differ. This is central to any comparison of the two educational structures. This is why it is so important to create a coherent model of the English adolescent's formative years. Of basic interest is the link between the family and the school. If comprehensive schools are going to produce change then they must create a new set of relationships.

Every society attempts to preserve itself but naturally the techniques of preservation will differ widely from one society to the next. However, central to the perpetuation of any society is its socialization process: the means by which the individual learns socially acceptable patterns of values, attitudes and behaviour.[1] It is not easy to make a

[1] There are several similar definitions. Elkin states, 'We may define socialization as the process by which someone learns the ways of a given society or social group so that he can function within it.' See Frederick Elkin, *The Child and Society*, New York, Random House, 1960, p. 4. Child has the same approach, 'The process by which the society moulds its offspring into the pattern prescribed by its culture is termed socialization.' See Irvin L. Child, *Italian or American?*, New Haven, Yale University Press, 1943, pp. 18–19. Looking specifically at political socialization Hyman concludes, 'One is naturally directed to the area of learning; more specifically to the socialization of the individual, his learning of social patterns corresponding to his societal positions as mediated through various agencies of society.' See Herbert Hyman, *Political Socialization*, Glencoe, Illinois, The Free Press, 1959, p. 25.

distinction between norms learnt through social training, and conformity induced by the presence or application of sanctions. In fact an integral part of socialization is learning the forms of punishment which society applies to its erring members.

Socialization processes are essentially conservative; they help preserve the society by fitting individuals into prescribed roles, and teaching them the values, attitudes and behaviour associated with those roles. The type of roles occupied will vary according to the individual's class position. There is, therefore, a close association between social class and role performance. Viewed in this light Plato's *Republic* is a classic socialization study. In his ideal state there is a perfect division of labour; the citizens are born into a particular stratum which they occupy for the rest of their lives. There is a sophisticated indoctrination campaign which ensures they willingly perform their designated tasks. Pre-eminence is given to the Guardians, Plato's ruling class: 'Gold and silver, we shall tell them, they will not need, having the divine counterparts of these metals always in their souls as a lawful god-given possession, whose purity it is not lawful to sully by the acquisition of that mortal dross, current among mankind, which has been the occasion of so many unholy deeds. They alone of all the citizens are forbidden to touch and handle silver or gold, or to come under the same roof with them. This manner of life will be their salvation and make them the saviours of the commonwealth.'[2] The collapse of the ideal state stems from shortcomings in its breeding arrangements: 'For your own race, the rulers you have bred for your commonwealth, wise as they are, will not be able, by observation and reckoning, to hit upon the time propitious or otherwise for birth, some day the moment will slip by and they will beget children out of due season.'[3] The end result is the ultimate disaster of discord: 'Then Rulers appointed from among them will fail in their duty as Guardians to try the mettle of your citizens . . . and when the silver is alloyed with iron and the gold with brass, diversity, inequality, and disharmony will beget, as they always must, enmity and war. Such, everywhere, is the birth and lineage of civil strife.'[4]

Most of the contemporary field work on socialization has been carried out in the United States and, as must be evident from the

[2] Plato, *The Republic* (translated by Francis M. Cornford), Oxford, The University Press, 1947, p. 106.

[3] *ibid.*, p. 263.   [4] *ibid.*, p. 264.

listed definitions, there is a strong emphasis on the continuity of behavioural patterns. The general theme of Greenstein's *Children and Politics* is that the most important consequence of socialization in the American context is to stabilize and maintain the political system.[5] Following in the same tradition, Hess and Torney claim: 'Of equal significance is the proposition that the socialization of children maintains basic values of the society . . . the values of the adult society are transmitted through child-rearing and other teaching practices to children who, when they become adults, reinforce and help to maintain the culture in which they live.'[6] In neither of these studies is there much concern with the social training of minority ethnic groups. In fact Hess and Torney deliberately excluded them: 'The purpose of this project was to examine the most characteristic forms of political socialization in the United States. To focus on this objective, it was decided to defer consideration of subcultural groups in which political socialization might differ from the dominant culture.'[7] Furthermore, 'Testing was conducted, insofar as possible, in city neighbourhoods which were not primarily populated by ethnic groups.'[8] This is a potential weakness; in order to present a balanced picture it is essential to be comparative. In addition, comparison is an aid in ascertaining the relative impact of the forces which make up the socialization process.

It is one of the common themes of educational sociology that the schooling system is explicitly designed to ensure the stability of our society. Rupert Wilkinson's analysis of the 19th-century public schools illustrates how they became the training ground of the guardians of the British Empire. The public schools opened their gates to the new commercial and professional classes, grooming their offspring for a variety of public positions both at home and abroad. The end result was a much closer alliance between the aristocracy and the *nouveau riche*, ensuring the perpetuation of many traditional values.[9] Adopting a much broader theoretical approach Lawrence Stenhouse has arrived at similar conclusions. He maintains that the primary function of education is induction into culture; the society

[5] Fred I. Greenstein, *Children and Politics*, New Haven, Yale University Press, 1965.

[6] Robert D. Hess and Judith V. Torney, *The Development of Political Attitudes in Children*, Chicago, Aldine, 1967, p. 7.

[7] *ibid.*, p. 229.　　　　[8] *ibid.*, p. 230.

[9] Rupert Wilkinson, *The Prefects: British Leadership and the Public School Tradition*, London, Oxford University Press, 1964, p. 4.

has a common set of cultural values which are introduced to the individual through education. 'The life of any group depends upon a core of common culture. From the understandings shared in this culture, people develop a set of expectations about how others will behave, and they rely upon these expectations to regulate their own behaviour. Any serious breach of such expectations by an individual threatens the security and peace of mind of the other members of the group with whom he is interacting. Accordingly, the group meets conformity to expectations with approval and reward, that is, with positive sanctions, and responds to breaches of conformity with disapproval and punishment, or with negative sanctions.'[10]

It is widely accepted that there will not be harmony in the social training of all individuals. Greenstein states, 'It should be made clear, however, that the effects of political socialization are not inevitably conservative, and the conservative effects of socialization are not necessarily desirable.'[11] Hess and Torney refer to the need for flexibility if the problems posed by social change are to be overcome.[12] Even Stenhouse is quick to point out that there is often a conflict between the cultural values of children and teachers; that adolescents are exposed to contradictory mores and it is not always the teacher's view which prevails. 'In the secondary modern schools themselves we find most children resistant to the education offered them, particularly as they enter adolescence. The academic subjects are not for them, as they are for the grammar school child, a vocation. The attitudes of the teachers are those of an alien social group. What the school attempts is eroded rather than endorsed by the adult social groups they will enter when they leave school.'[13] This pupil/school conflict is by no means applicable to all secondary modern schools and it certainly is not unknown in other sectors of the educational system.

A concerted effort has been made to examine a variety of adolescent viewpoints; to draw in those who are destined to become a part of the system, accepting most aspects of its structure and the way it functions; those who are likely to end up drop-outs in every sense of the word, and others who have an assured future as well as critical attitudes. Although in the same tradition as the work of the quoted American authors, the scope of this study is somewhat wider.

[10] Lawrence Stenhouse, *Culture and Education*, London, Nelson, 1967, pp. 18–19.
[11] *op. cit.*, p. 158.   [12] *op. cit.*, p. 5.   [13] *op. cit.*, pp. 120–1.

The Socializing Agents

Socialization begins at, or even before, birth. In order, therefore, to obtain a complete picture, influences which act upon the individual from his earliest days have to be considered. Clearly this makes the family the first agent to be observed, and many would insist that it also has the most impact. This assertion owes a great deal to the work of Freud who argued that the crucial aspects of personality are formed by the age of five. The factors he felt were especially pertinent evolve around the relationship of members of the family to each other; above all the way the child and the parents interact. At the root of this development is Freud's notion of the Oedipus complex. 'At the same time as his identification with his father, or a little later, the boy has begun to develop a true object-cathexis towards his mother according to the anaclitic type. He then exhibits, therefore, two psychologically distinct ties: a straightforward sexual object-cathexis towards his mother and a typical identification towards his father. The two subsist side by side for a time without any mutual influence or interference. In consequence of the irresistible advance towards a unification of mental life, they come together at last; and the normal Oedipus complex originates from their confluence. The little boy notices that his father stands in his way with his mother. His identification with his father then takes on a hostile colouring and then becomes identical with the wish to replace his father in regard to his mother as well.'[14]

In this research, family impact is seen in terms of a series of social, economic and political factors. Of paramount importance is the question of social class. When the sociologist is talking about social class he is invariably referring to differing family life styles; class and family are, therefore, closely related concepts. Albert Cohen stresses the hold of the family upon its members in these strong terms: 'His experiences in the family are the most important determinants of the frame of reference through which the child perceives, interprets and evaluates the outside world.'[15] He goes on to enumerate the values the individual has to adopt if he wishes to 'succeed' in American society. By 'success' he is thinking of advancement in the occupa-

[14] Sigmund Freud, 'Group Psychology and the Analysis of the Ego', in James Strachey (ed.), *The Complete Psychological Works of Sigmund Freud*, Volume 18, London, Hogarth, 1955, p. 105.
[15] Albert Cohen, *Delinquent Boys*, New York, The Free Press, 1955, p. 77.

tional hierarchy; obtaining a well paid, high status job. Middle class children are so much more successful than working class adolescents because their socialization experiences stress the correct values. On the basis of these contrasting class socialization patterns Cohen makes his evaluation of the location and cause of juvenile delinquency—it is overwhelmingly concentrated in the male, working class stratum of the adolescent population.[16]

There are few English studies of socialization which look at class in isolation from other influences. The usual link is between class background and the school; this is not at all surprising in view of the special relationship which has developed between them. The preponderance of middle class children in the grammar schools is explained by the support they receive from their families: the parents are interested in education and they encourage their sons and daughters to do well in their studies.

Many of the working class children at grammar schools come from atypical working class environments. Jackson and Marsden show that a large segment of the successful 'working class', grammar school pupils actually originate from 'submerged middle class' families. Their grandparents invariably held middle class jobs, and furthermore the desire for educational success was already present within the family circle. 'Thus there were a very large number of homes already educationally excited or thwarted before the birth of the child.'[17] The Middlesbrough and South West Hertfordshire study refers to a number of social characteristics which distinguish working class families with and without children at grammar schools. The former tend to have fewer children, more favourable material conditions in the home, and most important of all, parents who want their children to receive as much education as possible.[18]

There is a tendency for the educational level of the mother, the occupation of the father, and the attainment of their children to overlap. Douglas's survey showed: 'Education beyond the elementary level greatly improved the chances of men with working class origins entering middle class occupations. . . . Education, in addition, widened their social contacts; they were more likely to marry women who also had a superior education, and they were more likely to

[16] *ibid.*, p. 37.
[17] Brian Jackson and Dennis Marsden, *Education and the Working Class*, London, Routledge and Kegan Paul, 1962, p. 66.
[18] Floud, Halsey and Martin, *op. cit.*, Chapter 6.

marry into the middle class. . . . Thus the effects of education on social movement are reinforced by marriage, and this in turn influences opportunities of social advancement in the succeeding generation.'[19] There is a crystallization of influences: it is the socially mobile working class boy who intermarries with the middle class girl, and this assures the future educational attainment of the children of such marriages.

What is critical is the way class and school interact to shape the adolescent's occupational aspirations. Clements states the generally accepted position very concisely: 'It is clear that children of different social and educational backgrounds all tend to think in terms of different "areas" of occupation.'[20] Later he adds, 'The analysis of the jobs chosen, and of those mentioned to be avoided, suggested that these children did not choose from the whole range of occupations, though they may not have realized this—their mental endowment and their social and educational milieu have established, within broad limits, the particular segment of possible occupations in terms of which they think.'[21] Clements's evidence supports the Taylor argument that the secondary modern schools are geared towards training people for the less esteemed occupations; their pupils are fully aware of the kinds of jobs which are both available and unavailable to them.

Streaming is the one aspect of the school structure that has received a considerable amount of attention. Partridge, in a detailed study, attacks streaming on the grounds that it is a self-fulfilling prophecy: 'At the same time, however, the higher streams are invariably better taught. The boys who want to learn and who can learn more quickly are in the "A" and "B" streams; therefore for these classes a teacher's lessons must be more carefully prepared. Secondly, the work is more rewarding and the teacher is likely to put more into it, and thirdly, and perhaps most important, "A" stream discipline is generally good while "D" stream discipline is generally bad. Not only may promotion encourage a boy, but by climbing out of a lower stream into a higher one, he immeasurably improves his educational opportunities, and this may not be unconnected with the accelerated progress which seems to follow promotion.'[22] The main shortcoming

[19] *op. cit.*, p. 86.
[20] R. V. Clements, *The Choice of Careers by School Children*, Manchester, Manchester University Press, 1958, p. 8.   [21] *ibid.*, p. 11.
[22] John Partridge, *Middle School*, London, Victor Gollancz, 1966, p. 69.

of such studies is that they generalize from trends within one school. Although a large number of different sorts of schools have been examined, as techniques differ from one study to the next it limits the comparisons that can be made.

There is a neat connection between streaming and peer group culture. Partridge's work shows the presence of two conflicting peer group cultures within the same school and it is the streaming arrangements which mark the boundary between them. 'Each stream tends to develop its own attitudes and norms of behaviour like any school group; but since each stream is composed of boys of theoretically different levels of intelligence and certainly of attainment, then these norms vary considerably from stream to stream.'[23] This establishes a clear overlap between school structure and peer group culture, which is also supported by both Lacey and Hargreaves. In addition, influences accumulate: working class pupils end up in the lower streams of the secondary modern schools; they come from families in which there is little interest in education; high status future occupations are outside their realm of expectations; and finally the peer groups, which are invariably the centre of their lives, show a marked propensity to encourage delinquent offences. Most middle class adolescents proceed into the outside world by an entirely different route.

The claim that there are conflicting peer group cultures is not universally accepted. In *The Adolescent Society* Coleman comes to the conclusion that adolescent culture, at least in America, is sharply differentiated from the adult world: 'In a rapidly changing, highly rationalized society, the "natural processes" of education in the family are no longer adequate. They have been replaced by a more formalized institution that is set apart from the rest of the society and that covers an even longer span of time. As an unintended consequence, society is confronted no longer with a set of individuals to be trained toward adulthood, but with distinct social systems, which offer a united front to the overtures made by adult society.'[24] By way of further elaboration he adds, 'In sum, then, the general point is this: our adolescents today are cut off, probably more than ever before, from the adult society. They are still oriented toward fulfilling their parents' desires, but they look very much to their peers for

[23] *ibid.*, p. 75.
[24] James S. Coleman, *The Adolescent Society*, Glencoe, Illinois, The Free Press, 1961, p. 4.

approval as well. Consequently our society has within its midst a set of small teenage societies, which focus teenage interest and attitudes on things far removed from adult responsibilities, and which may develop standards that lead away from those goals established by the larger society.'[25]

Although Coleman accepts that there are a number of peer groups in each of the high schools he has under observation, the tone of the school is established by, what he terms, the leading crowd. This clique creates the norms which most of the other pupils try to emulate. Few of the trend setters have a strong attachment to academic values: 'As has been evident throughout this research, the variation among the schools in the status of scholastic achievement is not nearly so striking as the fact that in all of them, academic achievement did not "count" for as much as other activities in the school.'[26] He concludes, 'The relative unimportance of academic achievement, together with the effects shown above, suggests that the adolescent subcultures in these schools exert a rather strong deterrent to academic achievement.'[27]

At one point Stenhouse suggests that there is almost a universal teenage culture which is in conflict with adults: 'The teacher finds it extraordinary to face with equanimity the experience of the majority of adolescent pupils. Although the teenager's interest—sex, sport, money, possessions, religion and war, for example—are the interests of society (and of the teacher) as reflected in the press and films and for that matter in great literature, he handles them in a way which seems to challenge the adult society. Teenage culture, the shared understandings within which the adolescent discusses and reflects upon adult problems, is in its way a kind of protest flung by those who consider themselves to be grown-up at a society which denies them full adult status.'[28] This position is even more extreme than Coleman's for there is no recognition of the subdivisions within adolescent society. Furthermore there may well be this universal pupil/teacher conflict but, at the very least, it will take numerous different forms.

The interpretation of peer groups that raises the question of conflict within adolescent culture has far more appeal than the simple adult/youth dichotomy. This presupposes that there are certain well-established links between the adult world and at least sections of

[25] *ibid.*, p. 9.   [26] *ibid.*, p. 265.   [27] *ibid.*, p. 265.
[28] *op. cit.*, pp. 130–1.

adolescent society. Polk and Halferty, using Becker's concept of commitment, present a very sophisticated rationale for the potential dominance of adult values. They suggest that school success can take many different forms but attainment in one direction encourages achievement in another. 'Participation in student activities provides one of the clearest examples of this kind of bet. Once he becomes involved in activities, the adolescent adds a link to the chain locking him to the system. This involvement in activities gives him an increased stake in academic performance, since in all probability continued engagement in activities will depend to some degree on continued academic success.'[29] Holly's study of a London comprehensive school shows that it is the school-centred pupils who are most active in extra-curricula activities. Although in the English school, taking time off, for football practice for example, will rarely be dependent upon maintaining a certain level of academic achievement, it is reasonable to think of a close relationship between good classroom performance and high involvement in school sponsored recreation; both increase attachment to the school and consequently the values it promulgates. Polk and Halferty see a delinquent subculture at the other end of the scale from the system-committed youths. 'The uncommitted delinquent youth, it would appear, is characterized by behavioural withdrawal from the school. He does not study, he receives poor grades, and he does not participate in activities. This withdrawal tends to be accompanied by a concomitant withdrawal from identification with pathways to adult status as well, since the educational and occupational aspirations of the uncommitted delinquent youth are lower than those of the successful and committed non-delinquent youth.'[30] It is important to remember that both the English and American descriptions of adolescent society are referring to ideal types; these are the ends of the scale with most peer groups lying somewhere between the two extreme points.

[29] Kenneth Polk and David S. Halferty, 'Adolescence, Commitment, and Delinquency', *Journal of Research in Crime and Delinquency*, July 1966, p. 89. For an appreciation of the commitment concept see Howard S. Becker, 'Notes on the Concept of Commitment', *American Journal of Sociology*, Volume 66, July 1960, pp. 2–40. For another view, which also differs from Coleman's model, see Frederick Elkin and William A. Westley, 'The Myth of Adolescent Culture', *American Sociological Review*, Volume 20, December, 1955, pp. 680–4.

[30] *ibid.*, p. 93.

Measuring Influence

One problem, that is rarely faced, is the question of the relative impact of the socializing agents. It is comparatively easy to describe how two or more influences relate to each other but it is much more difficult to ascertain their relative importance. The first chapter discussed the close connection between educational reform and social change; one of the objectives of educational reform is to bring about certain types of social change. If this is indeed true, and probably few would deny its general validity, then it makes sense to know how much influence, if any, the school has in the shaping of children's behaviour. Besides knowing something about the extent of the school's influence it is just as important to ascertain the different directions it can take. The limitation of most educational research is the concentration upon patterns within one particular type of school. The shortcomings are compounded by the scarcity of analysis which relates the school system to wider aspects of the society.

The present debate centres around the possible impact of the school upon patterns of behaviour which have been formed at an earlier period within the family. Does the school have a positive part to play? Is it merely the icing sugar on an already well-baked cake?

Wilkinson's study of the public schools is one of the few attempts actually to assess the part the school plays in shaping career patterns. The public school pupils may originate from a select group of families but it is the school which provides the all important leadership qualities and ties of common loyalties. However there is no systematic attempt to verify these claims; his evidence is of a rather general nature which portrays the socialization processes within the public schools, and the careers of their pupils. Only tenuous links are drawn between them. Halsey, in a review of Wilkinson's book, expresses similar doubts: 'Certainly much more factual detail on the numbers of boys, from what social origins passing through what kinds of schools to what kind of careers in what periods, would have given the book a much more secure base for its delicate super-structure of description and analysis of collective states of mind.'[31] In a later work, concentrating more specifically upon the career patterns of Winchester old boys, Wilkinson goes part of the way to meet these

[31] A. H. Halsey in a review of Wilkinson's *The Prefects: British Leadership and the Public School Tradition*, in the *American Sociological Review*, Volume 29, No. 5, 1964, pp. 765–6.

criticisms; there is a genuine attempt to trace the connection between social origins, school experiences, and career choice.[32]

Douglas frequently touches on the problem. The second stage of
his study—the analysis of the national sample during its primary and
junior school years—concludes, 'The quality of teaching has a smaller
chance to influence the progress of the eight-year-old than the
eleven-year-old, and from this it would be predicted that the type
of school a child goes to has an increasingly important influence on
his performance, as he grows older. This is so; the schools' academic
record, from being the least important of four factors studied at
eight, becomes the second most important at eleven.'[33] However the
school does not appear to reach a position of dominance even during
the secondary stage of education. The subsequent research, based on
these later years, tends to ignore the issue. Instead there is a renewed
emphasis on the family: 'The additional information gathered
during the secondary school years, reiterates and underlines the
importance of the home in shaping educational attitudes and attainment.'[34] The school is now accorded a rather minor role: schools
with good academic records give invaluable help to intelligent pupils
from lower manual, working class families.[35]

Himmelweit notes that, '. . . the question we need to ask, and one
which has rarely been examined, is why the effect of home, the
principal socializing agent, is not stronger.'[36] Her brilliant article
illustrates how schools can structure themselves to raise educational
attainment in spite of unfavourable pupil intake. Of course the cost
is high; bringing some adolescents into the fold means that others
have to be excluded. One school, with an especially high percentage
of working class pupils, established a streaming system based firmly
on academic ability. 'The school in which streaming operated most
strongly was also the school which contained the highest proportion
of working class pupils. It seems that the school responded to the
challenge of its intake (whose norm would be to leave rather than

[32] T. J. H. Bishop and R. Wilkinson, *Winchester and the Public School Elite*,
London, Faber, 1967.

[33] J. W. B. Douglas, *The Home and the School*, London, MacGibbon and
Kee, 1964, p. 120.

[34] Douglas, Ross and Simpson, *op. cit.*, p. 177.

[35] *op. cit.*, p. 48.

[36] Hilde Himmelweit, 'Social Background, Intelligence and School Structure, An Interaction Analysis', in J. E. Meade and A. S. Parkes (eds.),
Genetic and Environmental Factors in Human Ability, p. 24.

stay the course) by creating an elite group within the school itself, thereby ensuring that, even if the school ethos could not touch all the children, a sizeable proportion remained.'[37] Another school, with a low overall ability level, made hard work the criteria behind its streaming structure. 'In this school, then, there were two inter-related indices of success; the assigned position afforded by being in the elite stream and the somewhat less important success position achieved through gaining the teacher's approval for hard work. As in the analysis of school A, so here too we find that these factors operate more strongly on the working class than the middle class pupils.'[38] There is an overlap, therefore, between the Douglas and Himmelweit studies in that both stress that the school can be more influential in the lives of its working class than its middle class pupils. On the basis of this evidence perhaps Himmelweit's initial assumption, that the family is the principal socializing agent, should be questioned. At the very least it suggests that the way the various socializing agents relate to each other needs to be carefully re-examined.

If the various socialization phases are logically connected then a simple model can be created.

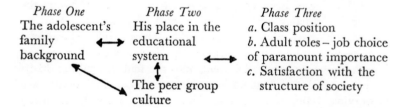

Phase One	Phase Two	Phase Three
The adolescent's family background	His place in the educational system	*a.* Class position
		b. Adult roles – job choice of paramount importance
	The peer group culture	*c.* Satisfaction with the structure of society

Clearly movement from one phase to the next varies from individual to individual. The fact that by law the child must attend school by the age of five determines transition between the first two phases. Of course there is no clean break; the family continues to exert its influence. The school leaving age provides a rough and ready division between the second and third phases. The model can be provided with a certain amount of flesh by tracing a number of alternate ways of flowing through its channels.

[37] *ibid.*, p. 31. [38] *ibid.*, p. 34.

Success stories

A. The adolescent comes from an upper middle class family, his parents are very interested in education and they frequently talk about school work with him. The home has what can best be described as a refined atmosphere. He passes the 11+ examination and attends the local grammar school. Along with most of his friends he is placed in the top stream and stays there throughout his school career. He steers clear of trouble with any of the adult authority figures: parents, teachers or police. Quite early on he decides he wants to continue his education at university; hoping eventually to follow in his father's footsteps by becoming a doctor.

B. This adolescent is socially mobile; his father is a skilled manual worker and wants his son to take advantage of the educational opportunities which were not available to him. Like the first adolescent he passes the 11+ and is placed in the grammar school's top stream. He soon leaves behind his less successful brothers and sisters, as well as his former friends in the neighbourhood. He is inclined to over-conform with the norms laid down by his teachers. He hopes to go on to university but he is neither certain of this nor of his eventual job.

C. Our third individual is an 11+ failure but his secondary modern school has an excellent reputation. Although his working class parents are not fully aware of the importance of education they certainly have no hostile feelings about their son's school. The boy does well in his studies and is selected to undertake a special GCE programme which has not long been introduced at the school. On leaving school he expects to take up an apprenticeship which will require his attendance, one day a week, at the local technical college.

Marginal individuals

A. Here is another potentially socially mobile adolescent. Although attending the grammar school he comes from a long line of unskilled manual workers. The family provides no support for his education; at one stage he was actually debating if it were really worth his while accepting his grammar school place. He finds the values of the school quite alien to those he has learnt at home. He slowly gravitates towards the bottom stream where his few school companions can also be found. Quite a few of his friends attend the local secondary modern school for he has not broken with earlier peer group cliques formed within his neighbourhood. He quickly grows disillusioned with the whole educational process, desiring to leave school as soon as possible. The teachers consider him to be a problem boy, and likewise think he should leave school as soon as the law permits.

B. At the best this adolescent can hope to maintain his family status; in fact there is a good chance he will be downwardly socially mobile. Both he, and his lower middle class parents, were hoping for success in the selective examination; he cannot adjust to the fact that he has failed. He becomes increasingly bored with his school, and envious of his friends at the more prestigious grammar school. His work reflects this boredom for it deteriorates as time passes. The final school year cannot arrive too soon for he is anticipating that his future career, of which he is still not too certain, will provide some atonement for the failure he has experienced at school.

The non-achievers

Although there are many different kinds of non-achievers one example will serve to illustrate the main points. The boy comes from a family in which the tradition is to earn one's livelihood through unskilled manual work. This is equally true of his father, mother, brothers, and sisters. He did not even bother to sit the 11 + examination as it was realized he had no chance of passing it. He readily accepts his low placement in the secondary modern school. All his friends live in the same district as himself and they form a well-known, troublesome clique within the school. Although he is occasionally in trouble with the teachers he is more inclined to accept the school as a tedious necessity. He is eagerly awaiting his fifteenth birthday when he will be eligible to enter what he considers to be the real world–the world of work. Everything about the school confirms his own assessment of his probable future role: the condescending or hostile treatment he often receives from the teachers, and the low esteem in which his form, 4D, is held by the rest of the school's pupils.

All of these movements through the educational system are ideal types but a survey of the literature suggests that they are based upon a considerable amount of empirical reality. At the same time, although this is not a complete range of examples, it does represent some of the most important flows.

Implicit within the model is the assumption that there is a well developed relationship between the socializing agents; that adolescents will flow harmoniously through the system. The fascinating cases are those where this does not apply. These have been referred to as the marginal individuals. Adolescents in these situations are subjected to a considerable amount of cross-pressuring due to the conflict between the social variables to which they are exposed. The concept of cross-pressuring has probably been most adequately investigated in the American voting studies. Berelson credits the cross-pressured voter with a very central social function, 'Yet viewing them from the point of view of the total community, they are in between the great voting blocs. They make up the social bridges between otherwise distinct and separate political subcommunities. Yet actually, such people, by being subject to the influence upon social minorities of different majorities, have more "freedom of choice" as to which group they will side with. They have no more freedom of choice on paper, so to speak, but their social location gives them more in practice. But this—which helps give the community a certain flexibility of political change—is purchased only at the price of high turnover or individual instability. Towns like Elmira are not one community but many divergent ones, and those who are in the position of bridging almost unbridgeable sociological gaps are inevitably ambivalent and politically instable.'[39] The cross-pressured adolescents can, therefore, be expected to show quite distinctive response patterns. Will they be the group most in favour of changing the status quo? Alternatively will they show the most diverse response pattern? Both trends are possible if Berelson's evidence applies generally.

Talcott Parsons is one of the few sociologists to think explicitly of the impact of cross-pressures upon adolescents. He initially assumes that influences which shape behaviour interact along carefully prescribed lines, in much the same way as the socialization agents in our model. Parsons argues that it is the cross-pressured individuals who swell the ranks of the dropouts: 'But rather than suggesting, as is usual on commonsense grounds, that indifference to schoolwork represents an "alienation" from cultural and intellectual values, I would suggest exactly the opposite: that an important component of such indifference, including in extreme cases overt revolt against

---

[39] B. R. Berelson, P. F. Lazarsfeld and W. N. McPhee, *Voting*, Chicago, Chicago University Press, 1954, pp. 131–2.

school discipline, is connected with the fact that the stakes, as in politics, are very high indeed. Those pupils who are exposed to contradictory pressures are likely to be ambivalent; at the same time, the personal stakes for them are higher than for others, because what happens in school may make much more of a difference for their futures than for the others, in whom ability and family status point to the same expectations for the future. In particular for the upwardly mobile pupils, too much emphasis on school success would pointedly suggest "burning their bridges" of association with their families and status peers.'[40] It is not an inevitable process; the upwardly mobile adolescent may well adjust to his school environment without any problems whatsoever and in doing so become just as achievement oriented as the most middle class of pupils. It is possible that there are special features about the home environments of such adolescents which distinguish them from their apparently identical rebellious counterparts. At least initially it is essential to suggest a variety of possible explanations for unexpected divergences.

So far all the examples of movement through the educational system have been taken from the selective schools. If it is correct that these schools have established very set flows then the problem facing comprehensive education can be reformulated thus: if the social and educational consequences of comprehensive schools are going to differ from those arising out of tripartism then the way the socializing influences relate to each other must also differ. This is why streaming is such a vital issue. It can re-establish all the traditional patterns associated with the tripartite arrangements. The central problem can be stated quite specifically: 'What are the comprehensive schools going to do for the adolescents from working class families in which there is little interest in education?'. . . 'Will the traditional non-achievement pattern be recreated in this new setting, or is the school going to provide these pupils with a new deal?' Naturally the comprehensive schools can introduce very important changes without in the least affecting these adolescents but these are the terms in which their success or failure should be judged.

There is one line of thinking which postulates that most working class children at secondary modern schools are also subjected to

[40] Talcott Parsons, 'The School Class as a Social System: Some of its Functions in American Society', in A. H. Halsey, Jean Floud and C. Arnold Anderson (eds.), *Education, Economy and Society*, New York, The Free Press, 1961, pp. 447-8.

cross-pressures. The implication is that there is a clash of values between working class families and the educational system in general. Michael Young claims, 'I have yet to meet working class people who decried the value of education, or did not wish that they and their children had more of it. At the same time they are often enough less than enthusiastic about the schools as they are now.'[41] This is similar to Stenhouse's argument that there are frequent clashes between secondary modern teachers and pupils over their respective inter-pretations of culture. There is some substance to this but all the evidence suggests that the most significant conflict between the home and the school occurs when the working class child attends grammar school. At the same time Taylor shows that the secondary modern school can gear itself to the interests of certain of its working class pupils. Then as in the grammar schools it is the more ambitious who, generally speaking, receive the most rewards. This is reflected in the introduction of external examinations which provide the secondary modern schoolboy with a real chance to atone for his failure in the 11+ examination.

The model provides a ready explanation of the relative importance of the socialization agents. Initially the family is most influential but as time passes the school increases its hold. The point at which the school takes over from the family will differ from individual to individual. Clearly some families exert a stronger hold over their children than others. All the adolescents in this study have been schoolchildren for about ten years, and for most of them family influences should no longer dominate their lives. There is still a need for more clarification: the broad variables have to be refined, the break-off point between family and school must be ascertained with greater certainty, and the ability of particular influences to retain a hold over localized subsamples requires further analysis.

As the school supersedes the family, so the work situation replaces the school. However, Stinchcombe maintains that it is the adolescent's perception of his future status that is the most important determinant of his behaviour. Juvenile delinquency, for example, is a response to the realization that all that lies ahead is boring and meaningless work.[42] This adds the concept of anticipatory socializa-

[41] Michael Young, *Innovation and Research in Education*, London, Routledge and Kegan Paul, 1965, p. 64.
[42] Arthur L. Stinchcombe, *Rebellion in a High School*, Chicago, Quadrangle Books, 1964.

tion to the discussion. It is not excluded by the model which poses two way flows of influence. Therefore, although at certain points in time some forces have more impact than others, the underlying theme is the way they crystallize into set patterns. In this way it becomes possible to incorporate future role perceptions in the analysis. Above all it is essential to move away from the simple either/or approach which has plagued so much of the past discussion.

3

PATRICIANS AND PLEBEIANS

It is relatively straightforward to show the connection between family background and school structure, the first two phases of the model. A number of questions, relating to adolescent attitudes and role aspirations, provide information on the model's third phase. Specifically the questions are:

Aspirations[1]	*Attitudes*[2]
1. Educational aspirations	1. Attitude to the 11+ examination
2. Job aspirations	2. Equitability in access to good jobs
3. Political aspirations	3. The responsibility of parliamentary democracy
	4. The nature of class relations

In conducting the survey a number of compromises have been made: only one age group, at one particular point in time, has been investigated; a number of socializing influences have been omitted; and there are limited measures of certain sections of the model. In spite of these limitations the survey did provide a comprehensive body of information, making it possible to look at a variety of quite complex interactions.

All the adolescents in this study were pupils in the fourth form of their respective schools when they completed the questionnaire. Nearly all were aged 14 to 15. This is an interesting stage in the life cycle; on the verge of leaving behind them the family and the school, and preparing to enter the job market. Even the adolescent who decides to stay on at school is being directed towards a general

[1] For the exact questions see the Appendix, questions 16, 31, and 51 respectively.

[2] For the exact questions see the Appendix, questions 25, 34, 54 and 62 respectively.

career goal. The past emphasis on specialization ensures that he will study a limited range of subjects, usually in the same area, and once this decision has been made it is not easy to change course.

They are also at one of the crucial points in the development of their personalities. Erik Erikson considers this age as the time when the adolescent struggles to form a meaningful identity, by searching to establish a satisfying role within his society. The major difficulties are encountered in the search for an occupational identity: 'It is primarily the inability to settle on an occupational identity which disturbs young people.'[3] This search for identity takes place during, and immediately after, the development of physical maturity: 'The growing and developing youths, faced with this physiological revolution within them, are now primarily concerned with what they appear to be in the eyes of others as compared with what they feel they are, and with the question of how to connect the roles and skills cultivated earlier with the occupational prototypes of the day.'[4] In the advanced industrialized societies the problem is compounded by the rapid rate of technological change for this makes it increasingly difficult to relate learnt skills to the occupational structure.

Erikson's work provides a link between the sociological and psychoanalytical approaches to the study of socialization. This stems partially from his stress upon the importance of adolescence in the development of the personality. It brings into focus a wide range of social forces, something which is missing from the Freudian emphasis upon the omnipotence of the first five years. For example, occupational choice is vital to the creation of a meaningful identity, and there is a wide body of research which illustrates the importance of the school in shaping job perspectives. There are, therefore, common problems being tackled in contrasting ways.

Testing the model demands a large, diverse sample. This provides one of the main departures from much of the related research. In the past there has been a tendency to favour the small-scale sample subjected to analysis through a variety of techniques. For this study it was imperative to have a large sample. The administration of questionnaires is one very efficient way to collect such a body of information. Face to face interviews give more information about

---

[3] Erik Erikson, *Childhood and Society*, New York, Norton, 1950, p. 228.
[4] *ibid.*, p. 228. Changes in the physiology of adolescents, especially the earlier occurrence of puberty, tend to confuse the relationship between physical maturity and identity crises.

certain respondents; those who benefit from the slower pace of the interview situation or alternatively require more explanations. Once the questionnaire had been thoroughly scrutinized, with the aid of a pilot study, it was decided to gather the evidence simply through their administration. It was possible to iron out the main problems to ensure the provision of more than adequate information.

The Pilot Study

The pilot study revealed specific objections to the questionnaire; most criticism was directed at the efforts to discover parental occupations and political affiliations. The parents themselves could have provided such information but this presents two important difficulties: it is time consuming and it removes anonymity. In order to cross check some of the information it was initially planned to include the pupil's name on the questionnaire. However there was a general objection to this, and the fact that anonymity was guaranteed later proved to be a strong bargaining point. The intensity of official hostility suggested that it would be rather futile to select the schools on any carefully prepared statistical basis. In the end schools who were willing to co-operate were included in the study; the main consideration was to obtain a diverse sample.

A short history of the data collection will best serve to illustrate some of the pitfalls which face the field worker in educational sociology. To conduct the pilot study one or two potentially friendly headmasters were approached. In fact they were not prepared to co-operate without the prior approval of the local education officials. The permission was not forthcoming and naturally there were the usual lengthy delays which occur when communicating with a bureaucracy.

Eventually negotiations with one Director of Education, and another headmaster were successful. The headmaster actually agreed to the administration of the questionnaire in his school without reference to higher authority! However, it was only after considerable persuasion that he sanctioned the questions on parental occupations. With the additional assistance of the secondary modern school in which I was then teaching, and the help of an excellent contact at a local grammar school, it was now possible to complete the pilot study.

Once the questionnaire had been revised the one co-operative

Director of Education was re-approached. No problems arose until a girls' grammar school, which had not been involved in the pilot study, was asked to co-operate. The lady chairman of the governors proved to be extremely hostile, not only preventing entry into that particular school but also influencing the local authority to adopt a more illiberal policy on research in its schools.

It was now necessary to revert to the policy of gaining admission through personal contacts. All the southern schools in the study were obtained in a period of six weeks; the initial breakthrough owing much to the fact that the author is a former pupil of one of the grammar schools. This compares very favourably with the northern experiences where it took approximately eight weeks to collect somewhat less information, and this after spending several months making contacts. The trouble with approaching the local authorities is not only that they take a long time refusing entry but also once they have made their stand all the schools under their control are out of bounds. A headmaster's refusal closes the door at only one school.

The majority of education officials showed intense, and often unreasoned, hostility. There was the occasional scepticism on the merits of educational sociology; the bias was in favour of understanding individual learning processes rather than the wider consequences of the educational process. A more general fear was the reluctance to allow 'outsiders' into 'their' schools. Of course headmasters may well be plagued by numerous requests to provide assistance for research projects. If this is indeed the case then reticence on their part is readily understood. However, discussions with headmasters did not suggest that this was a general problem and in fact it was unusual for a headmaster to reject outright an appeal for help; delaying tactics were much more common and this was often accomplished by suggesting that an initial approach should be made to the local education authority.

Reaction to the study differed from one type of secondary school to another. It was more difficult to gain entry into the grammar schools, especially the girls' grammar schools. It appeared to stem in part from the feeling that 'they had better things to do'. The secondary moderns were very easy to approach and usually quite willing to assist but their teachers showed the greatest doubts regarding the utility of the whole project. There was a widespread feeling that for many of their pupils the questionnaire would be totally meaningless. As was to be expected the comprehensive schools were far more committed; there was a demand that the results of the research should be made available to them.

These experiences are very enlightening in view of Michael Young's contention that there should be a closer interrelationship between research and educational innovation.[5] His basic thesis is sound: that far too much educational reform has taken place without first being preceded by careful investigation; that the research follows, often by a considerable time period, the innovation and by then it is far too late to change the course of events. For this relationship to exist the research worker must be provided with certain facilities and co-operation. The experience is that the parties most involved in introducing changes are also those most anxious not to be submitted to investigation. It was an especially difficult time to conduct research: the local authorities were subjected to increasing pressure from the Government urging them to submit their proposals for comprehensive reorganization. However, it is at such times that research is most needed. It has to be a reciprocal arrangement; the research worker has to be sympathetic to the difficulties facing the schools and officials. Nonetheless the absurd situation now exists in which the changeover to comprehensive schools is, in many regions, an accomplished fact but the research into their relative strengths and weaknesses is really only just commencing.

The large size of the eventual sample testifies that the obstacles were not insurmountable. The schools that co-operated willingly gave as much of their time as was required to ensure the completion of the questionnaire. It took most pupils one form period to fill it in and many teachers assisted me in supervising the whole operation.[6]

[5] This is the general theme of his *Innovation and Research in Education*.

[6] There is always the danger that the schoolchildren will put down replies which they think will appeal to their teachers. For this reason they were excluded, wherever possible, from supervising the administration of the questionnaire. However, this was not feasible in many cases as the pupils completed the questionnaire in their form rooms. In that case the immediate supervisor was a teacher with myself co-ordinating the total operation. Replacing the teacher does not automatically remove the basic problem; the schoolchildren cannot help but form some general impression of the person in charge of the supervision, and allow this to determine their responses. It is probably advisable, however, to have a stranger, rather than a known personality, in charge.

The Sample

A total of 1,482 adolescents—830 boys and 652 girls—completed the questionnaire. They are distributed among the various types of secondary schools as follows:

TABLE I

Distribution of total sample by school type[7]

	The sample			National distribution of 14 year olds		
	B	G	Total Ns.	B	G	Total Ns.
	%	%		%	%	
Grammar	18	14	212	19	20	114,584
Secondary modern	39	42	535	62	62	370,481
Comprehensive	34	37	468	9	8	49,583
Technical	0	0	0	3	2	15,607
Other	9	7	106	8	8	48,474
Total	100	100	1,321	101	100	598,729
Direct grant grammar			161			
			1,482			

Although not a representative cross-section of secondary school adolescents there is some rationale behind this distribution. The primary objective was to obtain substantial numbers in each of the main categories. Furthermore as there is special interest in the responses of the comprehensive school adolescents this is further justification for their inflated numbers. To ensure a sufficiently large number of comprehensive school adolescents for meaningful analysis, and still maintain a representative sample, would have required a very large scale study.

The first batch of data was collected from schools located in one

[7] The direct grant grammar school is not included in the main body of the table as it is very difficult to obtain comparable information for the nation as a whole. The figures for the national sample are for 1965, see Department of Education and Science, *Statistics of Education, 1965, Part One,* London, H.M.S.O., 1966, pp. 33–7. The 'other' category in the sample refers to one bilateral school and this same type of secondary school forms the major portion of the same category in the national distribution.

of the North's foremost industrial conurbations. The sample was then extended by including several schools in the Home Counties. Therefore, within the framework of the sample, there are adolescents who live in two very different parts of the country. Although the failure to set up a representative sample is a weakness, the research gains strength from its diversity. There is progress beyond the boundaries of the individual school, controlled by one L.E.A. The range of possible comparisons is quite extensive: between schools of the same and differing type, regional variations, and boy/girl contrasts, to name just a few.

TABLE 2

The Schools

School	Location	Numbers	
		B	G
Grammar			
1. Super Grammar (direct grant)	Northern Conurbation	161	0
2. Northern Grammar	,, ,,	36	0
3. Home County Grammar	The Home Counties	59	0
4. Southern Mixed Grammar	,, ,, ,,	25	42
5. Suburban Girls Grammar	,, ,, ,,	0	50
Secondary Modern			
6. Urban Modern	Northern Conurbation	54	61
7. Northern Modern	,, ,,	80	64
8. Home County Modern	The Home Counties	69	86
9. Suburban Modern	,, ,, ,,	31	40
10. Southern Modern	,, ,, ,,	27	23
Comprehensive[8]			
11. Northern Comprehensive	Northern County	85	77
12. Southern Comprehensive	Southern County	145	161
Bilateral			
13. Home County Bilateral	The Home Counties	58	48
		830	652

Wherever possible the direct grant grammar will be considered separately. This is because it is one of the most famous schools in the

[8] Southern Comprehensive is in a different Home County from all the other southern schools, and likewise Northern Comprehensive is in a separate county from all the other northern schools.

country, winning a high percentage of open scholarships to Oxford and Cambridge. It has, therefore, a national reputation for its academic excellence, the only school in the sample which could claim this honour. Its fee paying pupils, who form 75 per cent of the annual intake, are drawn from a surprisingly wide area; some pupils travel as much as 50 miles a day in order to attend. The entrance qualifications are stiff; the prospective pupil has to pass the school's own internal examination, which is more rigorous than the 11+. Most of the pupils have very definite assets: they come from families with much higher incomes than the average, otherwise they could not afford to pay the fees; they also have high I.Q.s, without which they could not pass the entrance examination. These adolescents are a meritocracy based on two pillars—brains and money. All these factors justify some distinct analysis. The one constraining force is the sparseness of numbers; this becomes evident when considering the impact of a combination of socialization influences. At times, therefore, it will be necessary to consider the two types of grammar schools as a single unit.

The regional item splits the L.E.A. controlled grammar schools into two groups. The three Home County grammar schools are situated in an area which is essentially middle class. This is only partially modified by the presence of a few post-war council house estates. These contain relatively prosperous working class families, the breadwinner earning his living in either one of the district's numerous light engineering factories or in a service industry. Northern Grammar differs somewhat from this pattern as it serves one of the older suburbs of Northern Conurbation. The differences are reflected in the buildings and their layout, the southern schools are favoured on both accounts. Naturally the class composition of the school is shaped by the district it serves; this means that the northern schools have a much more pronounced working class element. Four of the five grammar schools cater for just one sex, which is very much part of the grammar school tradition. The one grammar school which educates both boys and girls may provide some interesting comparisons with the other schools. One real weakness of the sample is the shortage of grammar school girls. This stems from the failure to gain co-operation in Northern Conurbation.

The function of the secondary modern schools is to educate the 11+ failures in their respective localities. Again what differences there are between these schools depends upon regional variations.

Urban Modern is situated in a decaying section of Northern Conurbation which is dotted with derelict warehouses and rows of slum
dwellings. In every sense of the word, it is a twilight area. This is a
very big contrast with Northern Modern, which is placed on the
western edge of the city and, in its new buildings, at least has the
appearance of being provided with adequate facilities. In fact this
may be merely a reflection of its more favourable location. The
southern secondary modern schools are found in the same area as
the grammar schools. Naturally they are far closer in appearance to
Northern than Urban Modern. Since the questionnaire was administered, Home County and Suburban Modern have been
amalgamated; the latter now forms the junior sections of the other
school.[9] The county is still trying to come to terms with the comprehensive movement and this is one expression of the attempted
compromise.[10]

Southern Comprehensive, placed in one of the many small towns,
between London and the south coast, has just over 2,000 pupils. It
is one of the few schools in England which could claim to be truly
comprehensive. Its pupils range in age from 11 to 18, and it takes the
whole ability scale appropriate to its locality, both boys and girls.
Before the introduction of a complete comprehensive set-up in the
town, there was a dual system of secondary education. One half was
organized on comprehensive lines, in the other half there were still
selective schools. There was no chance for gifted children to opt out
of the comprehensive system by attending the grammar school in
the other part of town. The only chance of escaping the comprehensive net was by paying for private education; obviously the cost
would be prohibitive for most parents. At that time there was still a
selective examination for the whole town. This was to enable the
comprehensive school, as well as the local education officials, to assess
the success of the comprehensive principle; this was measured by the
number of pupils who failed the 11+ examination and yet still went
on to pass several GCEs or proceed to further education. This kind
of success would probably have been denied these pupils if they had
not attended the comprehensive school. Within itself this is clearcut

---

[9] The junior school would educate schoolchildren aged 11 to 13.

[10] At the time of the study there were no comprehensive schools in this
county, and there is still no completed formula for solving the dilemma. It
appears that part of the solution may rest upon the creation of sixth form
colleges but so far these are not forthcoming.

information that the primary objective of this particular comprehensive school is defined in terms of narrow educational criteria. One of the easiest ways for a school to achieve examination success is to concentrate most resources on those adolescents who appear to have the greatest potential. At the very outset the school was in danger of becoming a super-selection agency.[11]

Northern Comprehensive highlights some of the problems, raised in the first chapter, as to the exact definition of the term 'comprehensive'. To all intents and purposes it is really little more than a large secondary modern school, for there is still a competing grammar school. This could not be classified as part of an approved comprehensive scheme under the terms of Circular 10/65 and yet at the time of study it was accorded comprehensive status. This is one indication of the need for deeper research into the range of comprehensive schemes in operation; not only to see the spread between the formally approved arrangements, but to see if plans, which on the surface appear legitimate, are in fact bogus. In view of all the differences between these two comprehensive schools it will not be too surprising if their pupils show very different response patterns.

The one bilateral school represents an earlier movement towards comprehensive education. Initially Home County Bilateral was set up as an area school: it was designed to educate pupils who had either just failed or just passed the 11+ examination. Grammar schools received the most successful pupils, the secondary modern schools the supposed failures. Rather than attempt to expand the school to make it comprehensive in the wider sense of the word, the authorities have been trying to change it into an all grammar stream school. This has been resisted by the teaching staff, which indicates that not all secondary school teachers take the grammar school as their ideal model. In some respects this bilateral school is more akin to the comprehensive ideal than Northern Comprehensive: it takes a proportion of school children who have been classified as of 'grammar school ability'; it has a sixth form; a substantial segment of its pupils pass several subjects at 'O' and 'A' level in the GCE examinations; and each year a few of them go to university. However it suffers from the same defect as Super Grammar in that the sparseness of numbers

---

[11] Jean Floud has argued that this is one of the dangers against which comprehensive schools must guard. See Jean Floud, 'Education and Social Class in the Welfare State', in A. V. Judges (ed.), *Looking Forward in Education*, London, Faber and Faber, 1955, pp. 38–59.

prevents much detailed separate analysis. In the few cases where there is a separate examination of the available information, only fairly general trends have been presented.

In spite of the reluctance of certain headmasters, in all the schools except one pupils in every fourth form received the questionnaire. Suburban Girls Grammar agreed to the completion of only fifty questionnaires, the process to be supervised by the school itself.[12] As the sample was short of grammar school girls, these terms were accepted. Inter-stream comparisons for this group cannot be made as the girls were instructed by the school to withhold this information.

In some of the other schools there were fourth formers who did not complete the questionnaire. There is the problem of absentees; the general impression, gained from my own teaching experience and supported by the observations of other teachers, is that most of these children come from the poorer segment of the working class. There is less support for education in these families and, therefore, less qualms about allowing their children to stay at home. At the same time they often face many social problems, and this fails to encourage regular school attendance. Furthermore the responses of one entire Super Grammar stream were excluded. At this school the distribution of the questionnaire, and supervision of its completion, was controlled by the staff. It was quite clear that for this one stream the arrangements broke down and the questionnaire was not taken seriously. It was decided, therefore, to eliminate all these responses. This still leaves a comparatively large group of adolescents from this school. As streaming is not based primarily on academic performance there is no special ability emphasis, one way or the other, for the remaining youths.

Empirical research results in a number of compromises and this study is no exception to the general rule. However the main objectives remain intact; the sample and questionnaire should provide more than an adequate base for examining those goals.

[12] This is fifty girls out of a total fourth form group of approximately one hundred and twenty-five pupils.

4

SOCIAL CLASS AND THE SCHOOLS

Class and School

The relation of the family to the schools is crucial to an understanding of socialization in England. The most important family information available to the study are parental occupations; on this basis the adolescents have been placed in a social class scale.[1] Underlying the concept is the claim that each social class has a somewhat different set of values. In particular there are varying levels of attachment to economic and social success. The middle class adolescent thus tends to come from a family environment where it is continually stressed that he should always do his best; the assumption being that there is not this pattern of values within working class families, or at least that the distribution of demands shows differing biases. At certain points, therefore, it will be necessary to control specifically for this item, which has been measured by parental level of interest in the adolescent's education.[2]

In the tripartite system the relationship between class and school leads to the following simple typology:

Harmoniously socialized individuals

1. Middle class adolescents at grammar schools
2. Working class adolescents at secondary modern schools

[1] The social class scale is based on the list formulated by the Market Research Society. The lowest point in the scale, which included old age pensioners and individuals in institutions, has been eliminated. In each case the father's occupation has been used to determine placements but where no information or inadequate information was given, then the mother's occupation has been used.

[2] For the specific question see the Appendix, question 24.

SOCIAL CLASS AND THE SCHOOLS

Cross-pressured individuals

1. Working class adolescents at grammar schools
2. Middle class adolescents at secondary modern schools

Verba refers to the cross-pressured adolescents as those who experience discontinuity in the course of being socialized: 'The socialization in social institutions at one point in the life cycle is inconsistent with socialization in another institution at a later stage in the life cycle.'[3] Naturally harmonious socialization implies continuity of experiences; there are few conflicting messages as the individual moves from one institution to the next. It is worthwhile to examine more closely the family background of the cross-pressured individuals. The potentially socially mobile adolescents will almost certainly come from rather special working class families.[4]

TABLE I

The class composition of the schools[5]

	Upper	Middle	Lower M	Sk. Work	Other Work	Total
	%	%	%	%	%	Ns.
Direct grant	12	43	35	7	3	161
LEA grammar	5	35	35	19	6	212
Secondary modern	0	3	18	42	37	535
Southern comprehensive	1	11	34	36	18	306
Northern comprehensive	0	2	17	58	23	162
Bilateral	3	19	26	26	26	106

Not only is the direct grammar school more middle class in composition than the other grammar schools but also it has more representation from the upper echelons of that class. In fact it is the only school with a sizeable subsample of adolescents from upper middle

[3] Sidney Verba, *The Comparative Study of Political Socialization*, paper delivered at the A.G.M. of the American Political Science Association, Chicago, 1964.

[4] The potentially socially mobile adolescents are the working class pupils at the grammar schools. For a discussion of the research see above, pp. 31–2.

[5] The boys and girls are not considered separately in the table. Any substantial differences will be noted in the text.

class families. In recent years there has been some debate as to whether this school should be included in the city's plans for comprehensive education. The defenders of Super Grammar, who not surprisingly favour its continued exclusion, often claim that the school already educates boys from a wide range of class backgrounds. This is perfectly true but there is nothing approaching an equitable class composition.

In comparison with either type of grammar school, the secondary moderns have an exceptionally high proportion of pupils from working class families, especially where the breadwinner is engaged in semi- or unskilled manual work. There is, therefore, a much more refined grading of class categories than a simple middle working class split would indicate. At the same time there is still the traditional overlap between class and school, and the number of adolescents subjected to cross-pressures is limited.

The class composition of all the schools, with the possible exception of Super Grammar, is influenced by regional factors. Certainly the schools in the North, both grammar and secondary modern, have more working class pupils than their equivalents in the South. The patterns for Northern Grammar and Urban Modern are especially distinctive; the contrast between Northern and Urban Modern is sharp, which certainly reflects their differing locations in the city.[6] Northern Grammar is the only grammar school outside the South controlled by a Local Education Authority. Whereas approximately half its fourth year pupils are from working class families, the figure for the southern grammar schools is nearer 20 per cent.

Regional location is also one explanation for the class disparity between the two comprehensives. Nevertheless it is certain the differing functions they are supposed to perform has an even greater impact.[7] The class backgrounds of Northern Comprehensive's pupils approximate most closely to those of the secondary modern adolescents. This is support for the initial claim that it is really a large secondary modern school; comprehensive in name but not in purpose and spirit.

Southern Comprehensive and the bilateral school have the most even spread between middle and working class pupils. In both cases this is to be expected: the comprehensive school takes pupils regardless of their academic ability, while Home County Bilateral aims at

[6] For a fuller discussion of this point see above, pp. 52–3.
[7] For a description of their differing functions see above, pp. 53–4.

the middle ranges of the I.Q. scale.[8] Southern Comprehensive is dominated by pupils from lower middle and skilled working class families. This is a good reflection of the town, which being dependent upon its light engineering industries, has an abundance of both skilled workers and minor white collar workers. Given the fact that to enter the bilateral school it is necessary to perform reasonably adequately in the 11+ examination, it is not surprising that it has a more substantial middle class element than Southern Comprehensive.

Based on the interaction between class and school, the following scale can be formed:

1. The direct grant grammar school is to all intents and purposes the preserve of the middle class adolescents. It is fully worthy of the title, Super Grammar.
2. In the L.E.A. controlled grammar schools the middle class adolescents still predominate but there is a strong minority of working class pupils. These are nearly all from families in which the main breadwinner is a skilled manual worker. Nonetheless it is a channel of social mobility for the privileged, or should it be the fortunate, few.
3. The bilateral school is split fairly evenly between pupils from middle and working class families. This is a reflection partly of its location and partly of the peculiar role it has to play in the county's educational system.
4. In Southern Comprehensive there is also an even class spread. There is not the expected preponderance of working class pupils, the town's economic base ensuring a large lower middle class stratum within its intake.
5. Northern Comprehensive is apparently comprehensive in name only; as nearly all its pupils originate from working class families the likelihood of widespread social interaction is ruled out.
6. The secondary modern schools cater for working class adolescents and a small number of middle class, 11+ failures. The class composition, therefore, reflects their overall low status in the educational hierarchy.

This is a straightforward confirmation of the findings of other educational sociologists. Although there are cross-pressured adolescents,

[8] As the school's intake is formed from those who either just pass or just fail the 11+, it really has a fairly high ability level.

with conflicts in their socialization process, they are very much the exception. The general picture provides a mere glimpse of the flows that are established in the schools. To present a more complete analysis requires looking at the further refinement of these flows by the internal structure of the individual schools.

Class, School and Streaming

The nature of streaming varies from school to school. Super Grammar streamed primarily on the academic interests of its pupils, rather than their levels of ability. In view of the type of adolescent who attends this school it would be futile to separate them along traditional lines.[9] All the other schools streamed by using ability levels but the actual number of gradations varied from school to school. Finally a three-tier hierarchy was constructed:[10]

	1st stream	2nd stream	3rd stream
2 stream schools: Northern Grammar, Southern Mixed Grammar, Southern and Northern Modern	1		2
3 stream schools: Home County Grammar, Suburban Modern, Northern and Southern Comprehensive	1	2	3
4 stream schools: Urban Modern	1	2–3	4
5 stream schools: Home County Modern and Home County Bilateral	1–2	3	4–5

[9] Although the grammar schools are supposed to educate the academic elite they still appear to require streaming. In such schools, therefore, the grouping of pupils into differing ability categories is taken to extreme lengths. Super Grammar syphons off many of the very bright schoolboys from the surrounding towns which leaves certain local grammar schools short of many talented pupils. In extreme cases they could lose one complete top stream.

[10] Almost any combination of the streams has its drawbacks. As the single largest group is the two stream schools, most comparisons will be made between first and third streams. This is a simplified picture of streaming within some of these schools. Northern Modern and Southern Comprehensive had two and three broad streams respectively with internal subdivisions, while for Northern Comprehensive nine streams have been condensed into three. In all other cases the number of streams is as listed.

TABLE 2

Class and Streaming[11]

	Middle class	Working class	Total
	%	%	Ns.
LEA grammar schools			
1st stream	75	25	75
2nd stream	65	35	23
3rd stream	75	25	64
Secondary modern schools			
1st stream	31	69	246
2nd stream	13	87	116
3rd stream	13	87	175
Southern Comprehensive			
1st stream	68	32	54
2nd stream	48	52	188
3rd stream	23	77	64
Northern Comprehensive			
1st stream	27	73	19
2nd stream	9	91	52
3rd stream	16	84	19
Home County Bilateral			
1st steam	73	27	47
2nd stream	60	40	20
3rd stream	18	82	39

The evidence illustrates quite clearly the hierarchies which have been created in the secondary schools. It is not simply a question of the allocation of working class children to the less prestigeous schools, for they tend to gravitate towards the bottom of the pecking order regardless of school type.

It comes as a surprise that streaming in the grammar schools does not appear to be prejudiced against working class pupils. This is not altogether unexpected; class bias exists at the point of entry and thereafter stream placement is probably based on merit. It is not especially meaningful to think of an equitable streaming structure

[11] Subdivisions within the two main class categories will be commented upon in the text as points of special interest arise.

when the initial intake is so overwhelmingly middle class. Furthermore, even if there is a noticeable number of working class adolescents in the top stream, they are nonetheless a definite minority. Over 80 per cent of the schoolchildren in the bottom streams of the secondary moderns, the two comprehensives and the one bilateral school, come from working class families. It is where there is a more or less even class distribution—Southern Comprehensive and Home County Bilateral—that the most clear cut link between streaming and class exists. Differences in the class composition of the first and third streams of these schools are significantly greater than elsewhere.

Research on early leaving from the grammar schools suggests that there is a clash between the values of the working class family and the grammar school environment. The adolescents in this study are approaching the minimum school leaving age and presumably the drop-outs are going to come from the ranks of the working class pupils in the bottom streams. These are the adolescents who will leave school at the age of 15, although the grammar school continues at least to the age of 16, the point at which 'O' levels are usually sat. However there are many teachers who feel that no grammar school education is complete without two years in the sixth form. There will be contrasting drop-out rates for the individual grammar schools, and Northern Grammar, with its much larger working class intake, will probably have the unfortunate distinction of heading the list. One indication that this will occur is the very marked class distribution differences between its two streams. The likely early leavers from the working class are isolated more carefully than is the case at the other grammar schools.

It is somewhat ironic, although not entirely unexpected, that it is the secondary modern schools which show such a definite tendency to discriminate against adolescents from working class families. In some ways this supports Young's contention that the values of schools in general are alien to the working class child.[12] However, contrasts in the streaming patterns of the adolescents from skilled and other working class families somewhat modifies his argument. In the secondary modern schools there are big differences between these two class groups, and as expected, it is the top stream which attracts the sons and daughters of the skilled workers. In effect, therefore, success at the secondary modern school is also dependent upon adjustment to an environment, and stream placement suggests

[12] See above, pp. 42–43.

that it is the children from either a middle class or skilled working class family who are most accomplished in this art.

In the secondary modern schools the top stream stands apart from the second and the third. Within these schools there are really two blocks of pupils, each composed of a very distinctive class make-up and separated by the formal streaming structure. The first block consists of the top streams and in these are found the few middle class adolescent who attend secondary modern schools, while the remaining pupils come predominantly from skilled working class families. The second block is composed of all the remaining streams with most of the pupils from unskilled working class families.

The secondary modern schools show considerable variation in their streaming arrangements, the actual numbers of streams stretching from two to five. In those schools with the simpler hierarchies the middle and skilled class element is naturally more pronounced in the bottom streams. In the schools with a four or five point scale there is a gradual decrease in the number of working class children as we move from the bottom to the top of the scale, and this is matched by a corresponding increase in the proportion of middle class children.

There is a good chance that adolescents in the favoured streams receive a disproportionate share of the resources available to the school. This may help to cement the ties between the school and the working class children in this favoured position. The values of certain working class children and those of the schoolteacher may well conflict, but this is not automatically an important problem. The difficult adolescent is likely to be quickly removed from the mainstream of the school's activities, and in certain cases even from the school itself. Once isolated from the mainstream he becomes immersed in a specialized peer group culture; he is now part of the anti-school crowd. This centre of antagonism to school values may find some support in the middle streams of the hierarchy, but it will be strongly rejected by top stream pupils. Partridge most persuasively presents the case against concentrating too many resources upon this top stream: 'The system cannot fail to depress the boys (and teachers) who are left behind. In the first place the boys have spent at least two years of their schooldays cramming for the 11+, or at least have been neglected for two years while their brighter brothers have been so prepared; a second failure, which is inevitable for four-fifths of the "second chance" candidates in this school, can only serve to emphasize the inadequacy of many of the boys in the school.'[13] It is essential, therefore, to be extremely careful about generalizations; even those schools which have been given the task of educating the system's failures are capable of structuring themselves to gain the co-operation of at least a segment of their pupils, and equally important, the parents of the favoured few.

Just as the overall class composition of Home County Bilateral came closest to that of Southern Comprehensive so the link is maintained for their respective streaming systems. Although the bilateral school supposedly selects only a narrow band of the I.Q. scale, its streaming is still remarkably class biased. In view of the trends within the grammar school, whose pupils are selected from only a slightly higher band of the I.Q. scale, this is totally disconcerting. However, some of the working class children come from rather special families. Close to the school there is a semi-permanent gypsy encampment and this provides the school with some of its pupils. Nevertheless, if this is indeed one of the county's moves towards comprehensive education then it appears to be little short of a total failure. If the comprehensive principle means anything then it certainly should not result in taking school children, with more or less the same I.Q., and separating them into different streams on the basis of their family background.

At Southern Comprehensive, the fourth form is divided into three blocks each of which consists of four streams, and positioning within a particular block is based on the school's perception of the individual's academic ability. Once placed in one of the three groups, streaming is by subject interest. The size of the blocks reflects conventional patterns: a small top group, a large middle group, and a small bottom group. It is hard not to apply appropriate labels: the elitists, the steady workers, and the outcasts, who are more politely known as the remedials. Movement between blocks is rather limited; the more usual tendency is for the adolescent to change from one stream to another within his particular block, in response to his fluctuating subject interests. Presumably academic ability is more constant than subject preferences.

Southern Comprehensive, which came closest to fulfilling one

---

[13] *op. cit.*, p. 60. The system to which he refers is the policy of spending a large percentage of resources on top stream, first year pupils. This is to ensure a high pass rate, in comparison with other local secondary modern schools, in 'the second chance' 11 + examination.

particular comprehensive ideal, has established the most clear cut relationship between the class background of its pupils and the streaming hierarchy. From the first to the third streams there is a uniform decrease in the number of middle class adolescents paralleled by a similar increase in the number of working class pupils. The only difference between this pattern and that of Home County Bilateral is that Southern Comprehensive includes a much wider range of the I.Q. scale. The traditional relationship between social class and secondary education is thus re-established in a comprehensive setting. In this respect there is an overlap between these findings and Holly's.[14] A very noticeable feature is the continued isolation of adolescents from unskilled working class families. Class placement alone would indicate that the comprehensive schools are not tackling the most important problem—how the system can best be structured successfully to incorporate those children with unfavourable home environments.

In Northern Comprehensive there is not such a sharply defined class separation. The competing grammar school, however, clouds the picture, for if there is a more confined social class scale then the opportunities for differentiation are limited. In the fourth year there are nine streams which have been condensed into three groups. Class distributions suggest that there are two distinctive blocks rather than a three-tier scale; on one side there are the top stream pupils, mainly from skilled working class families with the addition of the few middle class adolescents at the school, while on the other hand there are the second and third streams with the majority of their pupils originating from unskilled working class backgrounds. Once again this pattern most closely resembles that within the secondary modern schools.

What the class distribution for Southern Comprehensive suggests is that rather than substantially changing the relationship between the socio-economic structure and the school the comprehensive movement may well refine and reinforce the interconnection. To start with, there is a more or less even split between pupils from middle and working class families. Within the school they are streamed according to perceived differences in their academic ability and subject interest. In the top stream there is substantial minority of adolescents from working class backgrounds but this is more than counteracted by their almost complete domination of the bottom

14 For a full discussion of Holly's conclusions see above, pp. 23–24.

stream. The large second stream, acting as a buffer between the small elite and remedial groups, has a class composition representative of the school as a whole. In vivid contrast to this, Northern Comprehensive—both in terms of its overall class make-up, and its separation by class in the streams of the school—is reminiscent of the secondary moderns. Neither school appears to be fulfilling one of the major objectives claimed on behalf of comprehensive education: the integration of pupils from a wide range of social and academic backgrounds. Thus for many pupils the comprehensive school is very much an alien institution; there is a continuation of that tradition in which academic segregation also means class separation.

Working Class Social Mobility

The working class adolescents at grammar schools are potentially socially mobile; they have a very good chance of obtaining white collar jobs. To what extent, however, are they really subjected to cross-pressures? Are there any aspects of their family environments which distinguish them from working class adolescents at secondary modern schools? If so, what are these features and how prevalent are they? This is an attempt to establish the extent of the working class milieu which surrounds these adolescents. If they have so many special factors working in their favour then perhaps it is unrealistic to think of them as influenced by cross-pressures.

There are four factors, available to this study, which could modify the intensity of cross-pressuring:

1. Are the adolescents from skilled or unskilled working class families?
2. Is the family breadwinner either self-employed or an employee?
3. Would the mother's last job be classified as either middle or working class?
4. What is the level of parental interest in the adolescent's education?

The first three factors relate directly to the status of the parents' jobs. If the adolescent comes from a family in which the father is a self-employed, skilled worker and the mother has, or has had, an office job then he is in a very different family from the youth whose parents both work in the local cotton mill, operating a machine. The fourth item is a crude measure of the family's concern for the middle class success values. The latter of the two hypothetical families just described could be more strongly attached to such values than the former but this is not at all likely. Therefore, even for these 'breakthrough' items, there is a crystallization of their influence. They act as 'breakthrough' forces in the sense that they help the adolescent to overcome established social barriers.

The following table illustrates the total interaction of the four influences: skilled working class, father self-employed, mother engaged in a middle class occupation, and high parental interest in the adolescent's education.[15] Plus 4 indicates that all four forces overlap, Plus 3 that three of them overlap, and so on.

TABLE 3

The family environment of working class adolescents[16]

	Plus 4	Plus 3	Plus 2	Plus 1	Nil	Total
	%	%	%	%	%	Ns.
Working class grammar school	7	18	33	33	10	69
Working class secondary modern	2	4	18	45	32	420

It is evident that most of the working class, grammar school children have a number of special family influences operating in their favour. However it is important not to carry the argument to extremes. There are many secondary modern school pupils who have exactly the same features in their family backgrounds; almost certainly the crucial difference between the two groups is their respective I.Q. levels. At the same time there has been an over-emphasis on the special facets of the home environments of working class, grammar school pupils; it is as if there is a general disbelief that working class parents could possibly want their children to have a good education, or alternatively provide the necessary support which directs the child towards a grammar school education. Actually exactly the reverse is probably nearer the truth in most cases. There is a danger in trying to explain away all exceptions to an established pattern. It is safer, and more realistic, to accept that factors like a

[15] In Table 3 'high parental interest' equals frequent discussion of the child's school work; all other levels of discussion—'occasionally', 'very rarely', and 'never'—are equated with 'low parental interest'.

[16] The overlap is stronger for boys than girls but for both sexes the trend is still very much in the same direction.

high I.Q. or the desire for success are not the prerogative of just one social class.

The adolescents at grammar school with more than two variables modifying their working class backgrounds are very much a minority —25 per cent of the total working class, grammar school children. Furthermore there are still likely to be distinctions between this highly favoured minority and many of the middle class youths. The latter come from families in which there is a tradition of doing well at school; they are far less likely to look upon education as primarily a means of establishing, or increasing, social and occupational status. There is a family pattern of educational achievement rather than of all the aspirations being concentrated upon one bright child; this being supported by the type of secondary schools the brothers and sisters attend. The working class boy who passes the 11+ is often creating a precedent, the middle class child merely following a well worn path.

It is logical to assume that if the family environment of working class, grammar school pupils contains special helpful features then the middle class adolescent at secondary modern school should come from a family which, in one way or the other, is detrimental to his educational progress. There is an element of truth in this for most come from the lower middle class, and this is coupled with a somewhat lower parental interest in their education. However, the distinctions are not as great as between working class secondary modern and grammar school pupils, and furthermore nearly all middle class, secondary modern adolescents are in the top stream.

All the evidence presented so far shows that the traditional relationship between class and school is maintained. Although the comprehensive schools may alter the picture there is no substantial change. Introducing more detailed family information modifies the concept of cross-pressure but does not completely eradicate its utility. The sample has now been subdivided into the basic units of analysis for the following two chapters.

5

THE STRUCTURING OF ASPIRATIONS

The analysis of the adolescents' educational and occupational aspirations forms the core of this chapter.[1] The questions on educational aspirations are directed at the individual's desire to continue with his education after leaving school; more especially where this will be undertaken. Even the 15-year-old school leaver may be interested in pursuing some form of part-time further education. Although the adolescent who decides to stay on at school can delay making a choice, he is almost certainly thinking of some particular form of higher education. As current circumstances are pressuring the adolescent to make a decision about these issues they are, therefore, very much within his frame of reference. Finally no one could deny the importance of further schooling; education has now become the most prevalent means of conserving established status or achieving social mobility.

There are several links between educational and occupational aspirations. The amount and kind of education received limits the available job choices. At the same time the selected job may well demand more schooling. The 15- or 16-year-old leavers who take up apprenticeships, sometimes imagine that they have escaped the clutches of school forever, only to discover that they are now required to attend night school or the local technical college.

Politics provides a direct contrast with educational and occupational roles. A political position is something which few of the youths will have considered seriously. However this is supposedly a democratic political system, and in theory at least, political matters are of importance to all of us. Furthermore if the system is to continue, numerous political roles have to be filled. Therefore, in order to

[1] For the specific questions see the Appendix, questions 16 and 31.

provide a distinct contrast, the attraction of political positions will be assessed.[2] Is there a strong tendency for potential political leaders to be drawn from that section of the community with both high status jobs and a good education?[3]

Partly because of the large body of related research, it is relatively easy to predict the pattern of educational and occupational aspirations. However, the failure to select certain roles is open to various interpretations. The individual may not want to go to university or become a doctor on the grounds that neither a university education nor the medical profession appeal to him; rejection is not, therefore, a self-assessment of his own abilities, the realization that certain status positions are outside his grasp. All the evidence suggests that is not what happens. Aspirations are in fact a response to something more than personal preferences.

Political posts, however, are in a somewhat different category; the individual is not compelled to become politically active but most of us have to work and learn the skills relevant to our job. It is much more likely, therefore, that political roles may be rejected simply because the adolescent does not like the idea of being a politician and this, plus the paucity of relevant studies, makes it much more difficult to hypothesize the political trends. Given the contrasting interpretation of responses, the replies for further education and jobs should follow a similar course but deviate from the political pattern.

For all three questions the adolescent assesses his expectations as well as aspirations; it will prove fruitful to see how they relate to each other.[4] In all probability the responses will not show quite the same optimism as for aspirations. If this is so then it becomes interesting to ascertain where the decline in buoyancy is most pronounced: 'Is it more prevalent for one group rather than another?' Furthermore, 'Is it a persistent trend for all three sets of aspirations?'

Educational Aspirations

The first task is to examine the relative impacts of class, school and stream upon the formation of educational aspirations (see Table 1).

[2] For the question on political aspirations see the Appendix, question 51.

[3] In his study of the backgrounds of members of parliament Jean Blondel suggests that this is indeed what happens. See Jean Blondel, *Voters, Parties and Leaders*, Harmondsworth, Penguin Books, 1963, pp. 131–58.

[4] For the questions on expectations see the Appendix, questions 18, 32 and 52.

Although the working class boy was not disadvantaged by the streaming structure of the grammar schools, this is not reflected in his level of educational aspirations. There is always plenty of emphasis on the important part a grammar school education plays in assisting the social mobility of working class adolescents, but this information shows that within such schools class is still an effective determinant of aspirations. It is difficult to agree with Frances Stevens that, '. . . the modern grammar school is a great social unifier'.[5]

Rather than pointing out the impact of one particular factor it makes much more sense to stress the interdependence of influences. There are clearcut overlaps between the independent variables of class, school and stream which result in a patterning of the dependent item—in this case educational aspirations—along set lines. There is, therefore, a hierarchy of aspirational levels within and between the schools.

The very high aspirants, those thinking in terms of university or teachers' training college, are most in line with previous expectations. There is a clean separation of adolescents according to their school and class, with a less rigid, but nonetheless noticeable, ranking by stream. Home County Bilateral provides two upsets; the second stream adolescents have higher aspirations than those in the top stream and their bottom stream pupils appear to have less desire for further education than certain of the secondary modern groupings. The few middle class adolescents who are placed in this bottom stream adhere to the norms established by the dominant working class element. In effect there are two schools existing within the same formal structure; pro and anti school cultures which are defined by streaming.

There is not quite the same smoothness for either of the two alternative scales. This is because there is apparently very little grammar school interest in institutions of further education other than the universities.[6] If the grammar school pupil is not thinking of a university education then he has less interest in further education than either the top stream secondary modern or bilateral adolescents. This is applicable particularly to the working class, grammar school children and is yet another possible explanation of their tendency to

[5] Frances Stevens, *The Living Tradition*, London, Hutchinson, 1960, p. 261.
[6] Although the teachers' training college forms one category with the university its appeal is restricted mainly to the grammar school girls.

TABLE I

Further Education—The Tripartite Schools*

	University/ Teachers training college	Technical College/ Evening classes	None Listed	Total
	%	%	%	Ns.
Super Grammar				
Middle class	87	6	8	145
Working class	69	0	31	16
Suburban Girls' Grammar				
Middle class	67	14	19	43
Working class	(3)	(2)	(2)	(7)
LEA grammar schools *1st stream*				
Middle class	76	15	9	55
Working class	50	20	30	20
2nd stream				
Middle class	60	33	7	15
Working class	(2)	(1)	(5)	(8)
3rd stream				
Middle class	51	34	15	46
Working class	28	17	56	18
Secondary modern schools *1st stream*				
Middle class	20	47	33	75
Working class	7	46	47	169
2nd stream				
Middle class	6	25	69	16
Working class	0	40	60	100
3rd stream				
Middle class	17	25	58	24
Working class	2	25	73	151
Home County Bilateral *1st stream*				
Middle class	35	47	18	34
Working class	23	15	62	13

TABLE I—*continued*

2nd stream				
Middle class	67	25	8	12
Working class	(4)	(1)	(3)	(8)
3rd stream				
Middle class	(0)	(1)	(4)	(5)
Working class	3	12	88	34

* In this, and subsequent tables, brackets enclose numbers and not percentages.

leave school early. A grammar school education is so strongly geared to training the future university entrant that other forms of further education are either not made available to the pupil or come to be widely considered as undesirable.

It is important not to forget that the tables represent only the broad distinctions. Most grammar school adolescents are more desirous of becoming university undergraduates than students at a teachers' training college, whereas for secondary modern pupils the reverse is true. The teachers' training college is much more acceptable to girls than boys, and this is equally true for middle and working class children. This is partially a reflection of the fact that teaching is still considered by many girls to be a desirable occupation. In fact it is about the only job which offers substantial numbers of girls the chance of obtaining some kind of professional status. The girls also have less interest in further education, which reflects traditional societal norms. In the past a woman's place was in the home; not the sort of mentality likely to be stimulated to an interest in further education. There are also divergent patterns within the two classes. The information for middle class distributions is more applicable to the upper than the lower end of the scale. In the same way, the description of working class aspirations is more appropriate to those adolescents from unskilled, as opposed to skilled, working class families.

The differing class composition of the schools is reflected in their aspirational levels. The southern secondary moderns contain many more pupils who think about going to university than the equivalent schools in the North; the figures for Urban Modern are especially low. There are similar contrasts for the grammar schools but they are not quite as intense. These divisions may be accounted for by the stronger middle class element in the southern schools, but when controlling for class there are still slight regional variations.

The trends for expectations reveal that the decline in high aspirations is most pronounced amongst those groups least expected to record them in the first place. It is the secondary modern adolescents, plus those in the lower streams of the bilateral and grammar schools, who show the greatest divergence between high educational aspirations and expectations. The closest relationship is at the direct grant grammar school; these are the very youths who most want to go to university and in fact have the best chance of doing so. Looking at the less prestigious forms of higher education one can see a similar pattern. Naturally there is not quite the same steep lowering of aspirations, and at the same time the figures are bolstered somewhat by those who realise that in reality they are more likely to end up at the local technical college than at university.

Within the comprehensives the influence of class in shaping educational aspirations has greatly diminished (see Table 2). A comparison of the top streams of Southern Comprehensive and the L.E.A. grammar schools reveals complete class parity in the comprehensive but still big differences in latter schools.[7] Although Holly may be correct in stating that comprehensive education is re-establishing the traditional link between the schools and the socio-economic structure, the problem extends beyond this. In Southern Comprehensive a new elite, influenced by class at the point of entry but not in performance after this, is being formed. Holly was examining a London comprehensive where many of the brighter pupils can opt out of the scheme and this may account for this somewhat different assessment. In fact his conclusions are a much better description of Northern Comprehensive where the middle class adolescents are nearly all in the top stream and show a greater interest in university education.

If the two bottom streams of Southern Comprehensive are roughly equivalent to the secondary modern schools then there is an apparent increase in the aspirations of both middle and working class adolescents. However, this gain is completely confined to the large second stream; besides acting as a stimulant to the working class pupils it also provides a cushion for the not so bright middle class youths. At the outset this school was structured to fulfil narrow educational

[7] In Southern Comprehensive the working class boys in the top stream actually have higher educational aspirations than the middle class boys.

objectives and these it appears to be accomplishing but it does so at the expense of its social goals. Not one adolescent, Northern or Southern Comprehensive, from either a working or middle class family, who is in the bottom block of streams, aspires to receive an

TABLE 2

Further Education—The Comprehensive Schools

	University/ Teachers training college	Technical College/ Evening classes	None Listed	Total
	%	%	%	Ns.
Southern Comprehensive				
1st stream				
Middle class	61	17	22	36
Working class	67	28	6	18
2nd stream				
Middle class	29	22	49	91
Working class	18	30	53	97
3rd stream				
Middle class	0	60	40	15
Working class	0	51	49	49
Northern Comprehensive				
1st stream				
Middle class	33	29	38	24
Working class	15	31	54	67
2nd stream				
Middle class	(1)	(2)	(2)	(5)
Working class	6	54	43	47
3rd stream				
Middle class	(0)	(0)	(3)	(3)
Working class	0	13	87	16

education at either university or teachers' training college. There is, therefore, a very real separation of the talents. As on previous occasions there is an overlap between Southern Comprehensive and Home County Bilateral for in both schools middle class youths in the bottom streams appear to take over the norms of the dominant working class group. It is very unfortunate we have no information on delinquent behaviour; if this were distributed among the third stream adolescents, regardless of class background, it would be a good indication that the school is perhaps at least as important in certain respects as the home environment in the socialization process.

Just as the comprehensive school refined the distribution of the class categories by its streaming hierarchy, so the same movement takes place in the formation of educational aspirations. There is a small favoured elite, composed mainly of pupils from middle class backgrounds, but with all adolescents appearing to do equally well out of the school. The large second stream, consisting of almost equal numbers of middle and working class pupils, functions within the mainstream of the system. At the other end of the scale are the outcasts, nearly all from working class families, with little if any desire for further education. Of course this breakdown is true only of Southern Comprehensive. In Northern Comprehensive the presence of two blocks is reaffirmed: there are the top stream pupils with a distinctly higher level of educational aspirations than all the other pupils in the same school year. The tie up between Northern Comprehensive and the secondary modern schools is, therefore, more or less complete; the former merely extends somewhat the number of pupils who aspire to a university education.

The special points about the patterns in the tripartite schools can be transferred to the comprehensive environment: the top stream pupils think more about going to university than the teachers' training college, while the reverse is true of the other streams; there are the same splits within the class categories, between the upper, middle/middle and lower middle class adolescents, and the boys from skilled and unskilled working class families; and finally the decline in university aspirations is most marked in the second stream.[8] This second stream decline in university aspirations leaves the top stream adolescents at Southern Comprehensive in an extremely privileged position, for it increases the distinctions between themselves and all other pupils. Furthermore the same trend brings Northern Comprehensive and the secondary moderns even closer together.

[8] This is the difference between aspirations and expectations. There are no university aspirants in the bottom streams of either comprehensive school.

Occupational Aspirations

The major point of interest is to see if the logical affinity between educational attainment and job opportunities holds up in relation to these particular questions and this sample of schoolchildren (see Table 3).

There has been plenty of research on the impact of both class and school upon the formation of job aspirations; the general conclusion is that adolescents are realistic in their job choice.[9] This follows from the careful restriction of access to the necessary skills, for without such skills it is meaningless to think of high job aspirations. As Turner states, control in a sponsored mobility system is guaranteed, '. . . by training the masses to regard themselves as relatively incompetent to manage society by restricting access to the skills and manners of the elite, and by cultivating belief in the superior competence of the elite.'[10] Furthermore, 'The folk norm that defines the mode of upward mobility is the crucial factor in shaping the school system.'[11]

This research provides general support for the above line of reasoning. Class, school and stream interact to guide both educational and occupational aspirations along identical paths. A ranking of the high status white collar jobs would give rise to a hierarchy similar to that for the university/teachers' training college responses. In spite of this, however, care must be taken not to make too simple generalizations. There are still substantial numbers of working class, secondary modern school adolescents who aspire after white collar jobs and this means profesional and managerial positions as well as clerical and minor technical posts. Moreover this encompasses the young person from unskilled as well as skilled working class families. Although job expectations show a shift from this high level it is still not as marked as with the educational patterns. The problem which society has to face is increased: there are many schoolchildren with high occupational aspirations who will never be able to fulfil them. It would be interesting to see how they rationalize their failure; later evidence suggests they may well point to unfair biases within the structure of society.

[9] For an analysis of this literature see above, p. 32.

[10] Ralph H. Turner, 'Modes of Social Ascent through Education: Sponsored and Contest Mobility', in A. H. Halsey, Jean Floud and C. Arnold Anderson, *Education, Economy and Society*, New York, The Free Press, 1961, p. 125.

[11] *ibid.*, p. 121.

TABLE 3

Occupational Aspirations—The Tripartite Schools

	High status[12a] white collar	Low status[12b] white collar	Working[12c] manual	Other[12d] jobs	None Listed	Total
	%	%	%	%	%	Ns.
Super Grammar						
Middle class	70	5	7	9	10	145
Working class	56	13	0	6	25	16
Suburban Girls' Grammar						
Middle class	49	14	0	21	16	43
Working class	(5)	(0)	(0)	(2)	(0)	(7)
LEA grammar schools						
1st stream						
Middle class	76	4	2	2	17	55
Working class	55	15	15	0	15	20
2nd stream						
Middle class	73	7	13	7	0	15
Working class	(3)	(2)	(3)	(0)	(0)	(8)
3rd stream						
Middle class	49	19	9	17	9	46
Working class	39	17	6	11	28	18
Secondary modern schools						
1st stream						
Middle class	20	27	12	31	11	75
Working class	24	29	20	15	11	169
2nd stream						
Middle class	19	25	25	25	6	16
Working class	5	23	40	19	13	100

[12a] High status white collar: the professions, top administrative and executive posts, research, teaching and high technical positions.

[12b] Low status white collar: clerical, minor administrative and technical jobs.

[12c] Working manual: skilled and unskilled working class jobs; for the girls this would include hairdressing, machining, mill work and certain of the shop jobs.

[12d] Other: composed mainly of the glamour jobs: sportsman for the boys; actress and model for the girls.

TABLE 3 – *continued*

3rd stream						
Middle class	17	13	42	8	21	24
Working class	9	21	41	7	23	151
Home County Bilateral						
1st stream						
Middle class	56	15	9	21	0	34
Working class	23	23	23	8	23	13
2nd stream						
Middle class	50	17	0	25	8	12
Working class	(2)	(2)	(1)	(1)	(2)	(8)
3rd stream						
Middle class	(1)	(2)	(2)	(0)	(0)	(5)
Working class	12	15	26	21	26	34

The boys record the overwhelming majority of the replies placed in the 'working manual' category. There is little interest, however, in unskilled manual work for nearly all the selected jobs require at least a minimum of skills. A comparison of the boys' responses for the 'low status white collar' and 'working manual' jobs gives rise to some important points. In practically every case there is more attraction towards the working class jobs.[13] The most obvious differences, therefore, between the groups are in terms of occupations which have been listed as 'high status white collar'. Glass and Hall's research into actual patterns of social mobility concludes that education reinforces, rather than substantially alters, the impact of other socialization agents, and where there is upward mobility it is of a rather limited nature – movement from a working class background into the lower middle class.[14] In other words their mobility is accomplished by stepping into the very jobs which are least attractive to the majority of them.

Undoubtedly the most unrealistic aspirations are those placed in the 'other' category. For the most part this consists of a variety of glamour jobs which are especially appealing to the girls, and this

[13] The one exception is the working class boys at Super Grammar.

[14] D. V. Glass and J. R. Hall, 'A Study of Inter-Generational Changes in Status' and 'Education and Social Mobility' in D. V. Glass (ed.), *Social Mobility in Great Britain*, London, Routledge and Kegan Paul, pp. 177–217, and 291–307.

is true regardless of their class background or the type of school they attend. For the boys these jobs have a more specialized attraction: it is confined to the secondary moderns, and the bottom streams of the grammar and bilateral schools. It is not easy to establish why this should be so but it is possible to surmise that it represents a reaction against the humdrum jobs they will almost certainly end up doing. Few adolescents actually *expect* to take up such jobs, which once again shows their accurate perception of the available opportunities. At the same time it suggests that many of the usual avenues of advance are not very appealing to them.

TABLE 4

Occupational Aspirations— The Comprehensive Schools

	High status white collar	Low status white collar	Working manual	Other jobs	None Listed	Total
	%	%	%	%	%	Ns.
Southern Comprehensive						
1st stream						
Middle class	50	11	3	14	22	36
Working class	50	6	0	28	17	18
2nd stream						
Middle class	35	18	8	21	18	91
Working class	27	26	11	23	13	97
3rd stream						
Middle class	7	40	13	20	20	15
Working class	6	37	25	18	14	49
Northern Comprehensive						
1st stream						
Middle class	50	17	8	8	17	24
Working class	31	21	10	24	13	67
2nd stream						
Middle class	(2)	(2)	(1)	(0)	(0)	(5)
Working class	34	32	9	17	9	47
3rd stream						
Middle class	(0)	(1)	(0)	(0)	(2)	(3)
Working class	0	19	25	6	50	16

The link between educational and occupational aspirations is closer for the comprehensive than the selective system adolescents. At Southern Comprehensive there is not a gradual decline in the level of 'high status white collar' aspirations from the top to the bottom streams. The bottom streams differ so radically that they form a separate school within the school. Nevertheless it is still meaningful to think of three distinctive strata, for the top stream pupils are still in a privileged position. Other similarities remain intact: the distance between the schools, the narrowing of class distinctions within the streams, the important position of the middle block at Southern Comprehensive, and the central issue of the refinement of flows through the school.

Because the adolescents are more neatly separated into distinct groups there is more realism in their choice of jobs. Few of them, regardless of class background or school, who are pupils in the third stream, aspire to jobs at the top of the prestige scale. In the case of the only exception, the second stream pupils of Northern Comprehensive, they melt away at the level of expectations. Further comparisons with the tripartite school hold good: the preference of the boys for 'working manual' as opposed to 'low status white collar' jobs, the selection of skilled rather than unskilled manual work, and finally the much stronger appeal of the glamour jobs to the girls in general and the boys of the lower streams.

The overall distribution for occupational and educational aspirations is very similar. However, for some individuals the job market represents the chance to atone for an unrewarding educational career. In fact there is far more realism about further education than future jobs. It can only be hoped, but not really expected, that a new period of frustration will not develop.

Political Roles

There is contradictory evidence on the interdependence of class and political positions. Blondel maintains, 'Whether one likes it or not, politics is a middle class job and the training appropriate for middle class jobs is also training for politics. The dice are loaded by the present structure of society as well as by the natural conditions which govern the job of politics in any society.'[15] Blondel is thinking of the member of parliament, who puts up for election, who is elected

[15] *op. cit.*, p. 133.

and who has become a minister. In each case the middle class element increases in prevalence. For the main parliamentary parties he reaches the following conclusion: 'Some manual groups may be represented in the parliamentary Labour party, but the middle class as a whole is over-represented in both parliamentary parties. The higher one is in the social scale, the better chance one has of finding a good seat, unless, in the Labour party, one happens to be in a union which customarily sponsors many seats. There is thus a superficial similarity between the Conservative and Labour parliamentary parties. Labour may find place for about ninety workers and the Conservatives for only one; but Labour has many more manual workers among its electors and among its members than among its M.P.s.'[16] The Labour Party has approximately twice as many working class voters as the Conservative party, but it has ninety times as many working class M.P.s. Therefore, even on the basis of his own figures there is not quite the similarity between the class composition of the two two main parliamentary parties as Blondel would have us believe.

The implication of Blondel's research is that it would be highly unrealistic of the working class child to form any political aspirations. The Barking study of local councillors, however, presents a somewhat different picture. Certainly the middle class occupations are over-represented on the council: 'In contrast, middle class representation on the council (35 per cent) exceeds the proportion of middle class persons (10 per cent) by three times.'[17] The situation, however, is far less extreme than that described by Blondel: 'It will be observed that exactly two-thirds of the members are working class (i.e., fall into groups 3, 4, and 5). . . .'[18]

The contrast between Barking Town Hall and the House of Commons is repeated for the educational background of their respective members. The composition of the Conservative parliamentary party is basically public school, with a substantial minority of ex-grammar school boys, but with hardly any representatives from the elementary and secondary modern schools. In the Labour parliamentary party there is a more even distribution between the varying types of secondary schools. Therefore, even at this high

[16] op. cit., pp. 139–40.
[17] A. M. Rees and T. Smith, *Town Councillors: A Study of Barking*, London, Action Trust Society, 1965, pp. 19–20.
[18] ibid., p. 19.

altitude the Labour party is a vehicle of social mobility for a few individuals. In Barking we find, 'The formal schooling of the majority of the members of Barking Council was brief and limited in scope. Two-thirds of all the councillors—and three-quarters of the Labour group—attended elementary school only.'[19]

Blondel may be correct in stating that to be successful in politics requires the possession of certain middle class skills but his concentration upon the House of Commons appears to blind him to the fact that politics is also a channel of mobility as well as a means of affirming traditional status. In addition it has to be remembered that there are far more political positions at the local level. The evidence of the present research is inclined to support the Barking study; political positions are more attractive to the middle class segment of the sample but this does not prevent a significant minority of working class adolescents having aspirations in this direction.

The most striking feature of Table 5 is its radical departure from previous patterns. For the adminisive posts there is a slight tendency for the middle class and grammar school respondents to have higher aspirations than the working class and secondary modern youths, but even this narrow distinction disappears with the elected positions. The really important point is that for expectations the relative distributions remain approximately the same.[20] In other words for many working class adolescents political positions are still within their frame of reference, even if they attend the less prestigious secondary schools. The narrowing of the distance between the various groups occurs because the middle class, grammar school pupils do not really find the listed political roles particularly attractive; the administrative posts, which are only marginally political, are more appealing to them. It is fair to say that there is no group which has an outstanding interest in politics judged according to this criteria.

Certain comparisons can be made with the American experience. There attention has been centred upon the political activity of minority ethnic groups.[21] Robert Lane presents some conflicting

[19] *ibid.*, p. 16.
[20] However, it is necessary to keep in mind that the two questions differed somewhat.
[21] For a good study of the political activities of a variety of ethnic groups see Robert A. Dahl, *Who Governs?*, New Haven, Yale University Press, 1960.

TABLE 5

Political Aspirations – The Tripartite Schools[22]

	Elective: M.P. or Local Councillor	Administrative: London Civil Servant or Local Clerk	None	Total
	%	%	%	Ns.
Super Grammar				
Middle class	34	14	51	145
Working class	50	13	38	16
Suburban Girls Grammar				
Middle class	44	19	38	43
Working class	(0)	(2)	(5)	(7)
LEA grammar schools				
1st stream				
Middle class	18	24	58	55
Working class	35	10	55	20
2nd stream				
Middle class	27	33	40	15
Working class	(3)	(0)	(5)	(8)
3rd stream				
Middle class	20	28	52	46
Working class	17	17	67	18
Secondary modern schools				
1st stream				
Middle class	24	19	57	75
Working class	14	17	69	169
2nd stream				
Middle class	13	13	75	16
Working class	15	9	76	100
3rd stream				
Middle class	42	17	42	24
Working class	13	7	81	151

[22] In spite of the distinction between the Houses of Parliament and the local town hall, the division in the table is between elective and administrative posts. Actually few of the adolescents selected the local councillor option.

TABLE 5–*continued*

Home County Bilateral				
1st stream				
Middle class	24	21	56	34
Working class	23	23	54	13
2nd stream				
Middle class	8	17	75	12
Working class	(3)	(3)	(2)	(8)
3rd stream				
Middle class	(1)	(0)	(4)	(5)
Working class	26	6	68	34

information on the problem: 'Unlike subordinate class status, ethnic status, in general, is unlikely to depress political interest', but he continues, 'Membership in an ethnic group produces attitudes, and indeed qualities of personality, which have a bearing on the social and political participation of the individual; among these is the sense of subordinate status, the feeling that society undervalues the individual and his group, or at least the feeling that they are constantly on trial.'[23] The end result is apathy, hedonism, living for the moment, expectations of other worldly rewards, and low political participation.

It is probably realistic to perceive subordinate class status in this country, and subordinate ethnic status in the United States, as generally depressing political activity and interest. At the same time politics acts as a very real channel of mobility for the individual with high political motivation. The social and political structures of the two countries make this possible: the urban concentration of the ethnic population of the United States and the organization of the trade unions in this country. Obviously educational attainment is still the major route to social advancement for most working class boys but politics is a possible alternative for a few of them.

Table 6 provides another strong overlap with the patterns in tripartite schools. While in Southern Comprehensive there is still the streaming hierarchy for the 'elective' positions it is nowhere near as evident as with the previous data. With expectations there is a pronounced, but consistent, lowering of aspirations across all the classes. The overall conclusion, therefore, must be that although

[23] *op. cit.*, p. 235 (1st quote), and p. 251 (2nd quote).

political roles are within the compass of a substantial minority of adolescents, and neither class nor school appears to be important in determining this, for the overwhelming majority there is neither the wish to attain such positions not the expectation that individuals like themselves could actually do so.

TABLE 6

Political Aspirations—The Comprehensive Schools

	Elective M.P./Local Councillor	Administrative London Civil Servant Local clerk	None	Total
	%	%	%	ns.
Southern Comprehensive				
1st stream				
Middle class	33	14	53	36
Working class	22	11	67	18
2nd stream				
Middle class	17	13	70	91
Working class	16	18	87	97
3rd stream				
Middle class	13	13	73	15
Working class	18	18	63	49
Northern Comprehensive				
1st stream				
Middle class	13	33	54	24
Working class	48	16	36	67
2nd stream				
Middle class	(1)	(1)	(3)	(5)
Working class	30	23	47	47
3rd stream				
Middle class	(0)	(0)	(3)	(3)
Working class	44	13	44	16

Conclusions

The study shows how the internal streaming of the individual comprehensive schools reintroduces most of the old rigidities: segregation according to social origins and academic ability. It is not at all surprising, therefore, that the distribution of aspirations for the tripartite and comprehensive schools is remarkably similar. Nevertheless the two comprehensive schools did result in a somewhat distinctive patterning of aspirations—both from the selective secondary schools and from each other. Class is not such a constraining force in the comprehensive milieu; the adolescents who enter the top stream form something of a true meritocracy. The fact that a middle class background greatly helps in entering this stream somewhat sours the possible gain. However throughout the streams, class differences are not as great as in the selective schools. It is apparent that the comprehensive schools have as their primary objective the functions of a super-selection agency rather than the initiation of far reaching social change.

This basic conclusion is confirmed by the part played by the large second stream at Southern Comprehensive. Educational and occupational aspirations in this stream were noticeably higher than for the equivalent groups in the secondary modern schools. It therefore provides a real extension of opportunities by bringing aspirations into the focus of both working class and middle class youths. It presents opportunities which may well have been denied them if they had attended a secondary modern school. Even Northern Comprehensive succeeds in raising aspirational levels higher than the secondary modern schools; here it is the top streams which undertake this task.

What has to be asked is: 'Are these gains sufficient to justify the cost of introducing comprehensive education?' Before answering this question it is imperative to think of the price which has to be paid for these limited gains. A certain segment of the population has to pay the cost of this innovation. Selection and segregation can be equally rigid within either of the two schooling systems; in the comprehensive schools the outcast group is more narrowly defined but nonetheless it still exists. In some ways there is less motivation on the part of these pupils for they record fewer high aspirations than any other subsample. This is true for both the middle and working class adolescents and lies at the heart of the refining of socialization flows. Although this is not applicable to the political information, the special factors in this case do not detract from the main thesis. It is not that the political patterns upset trends within the comprehensive schools alone but that they in fact change them throughout the sample, and furthermore the changes are in the same direction regardless of the type of school under observation.

6

THE HOME AND THE
SCHOOL

Most work on this subject has stressed the over-riding importance of the family in the socialization process. In this book an alternate position has been put forward: it is more realistic to see how various socialization agents—for example the family and the school—interrelate to pattern adolescent behaviour. At some point in time, however, it is necessary to consider the relative importance of variables. In Chapter Two a theoretical solution was suggested; it is now time to propose more concrete measures.

Besides the work of Douglas there have been few attempts to compare systematically the impact of the family and the school in the socialization process.[1] Few researchers view the development of the individual in complex terms; they are inclined to stress the importance of just one set of agents whether it be the family, school or peer groups. As well as starting with limited theoretical perspectives, past research has generally suffered from methodological limitations: small samples, confined to one school with little diversity in their social composition.

In this chapter, using the simple chi square test, aspirations will be correlated with:

1. *The Family*
   The contrast is between middle and working class adolescents.
2. *The Schools*
   The comprehensive and tripartite schools will be considered separately. L.E.A. controlled grammar schools and the secondary

---

[1] For a review of Douglas's conclusions see above, p. 37.

moderns provide the comparisons in the tripartite system, while Southern Comprehensive represents the comprehensive schools.[2]

3. *Streaming*

In Southern Comprehensive the three tier hierarchy is a perfectly adequate basis for streaming comparisons. As many of the tripartite secondary schools have only two streams comparisons will be made between the top streams as opposed to the second and third streams.[3]

When a particular correlation is made—for example between social class and educational aspirations—there will be controls on school and streaming. The objective, therefore, is to measure the significance of the relationship between two variables while controlling for two other items.[4] If social class and educational aspirations are correlated then the following combinations arise:

The Variables:

Independent	*Control*[5]	*Dependent*[6]
Middle and working class comparisons	1. Top stream, grammar	Educational aspirations
	2. 2nd/3rd stream, grammar	
	3. Top stream, secondary modern	
	4. 2nd/3rd stream, secondary modern	

[2] The direct grant grammar has been excluded as there is no comparable streaming information for this school. As Northern Comprehensive was creamed of its brightest pupils it cannot really be used as a fair example of comprehensive education.

[3] For a more complete picture of streaming in the schools see above, pp. 60–6. Due to the lack of streaming information Suburban Girls' Grammar has been excluded.

[4] The technique, the additive properties of chi square, is referred to in nearly all the statistical textbooks. See A. Bradford Hill, *Principles of Medical Statistics*, London, Lancet Ltd., 1961, p. 174. The chi square test,

$$\chi^2 = \sum \frac{(o-e)^2}{e}$$

assumes a nul hypothesis has been posed, e.g. social class will not influence the patterns of educational aspirations. The greater the chi square value the more unlikely it is that the nul hypothesis is correct. The usual level of significance—$p = 0.05$—has been used.

[5] Only the tripartite schools are referred to in this example, the comprehensive adolescents will be analysed separately.

[6] In each case there will be a simple two point scale, 'high' and 'low' based

There are, therefore, four situations in which the impact of class upon educational aspirations has to be considered. Once the chi square value for each case has been computed, they must be totalled along with the degrees of freedom. This provides the total chi square value with class as the independent variable. When school is the independent variable then the controls are for class and stream. Finally streaming takes the place of school, controlling now for school and social class. The total chi square values can then be compared; with one or two reservations, best left to the presentation of the analysis, the higher the total chi square value the more significant is the impact of that socialization agent upon status aspirations (the dependent items in this chapter).

Educational Aspirations

Significant Differences[7]

	Tripartite Schools	Southern Comprehensive
Class	0·01	Not significant
School	0·01	Not applicable
Streaming	0·01	0·01

The most striking feature is the contrasting importance of class within the two educational systems. This completely verifies the earlier statements. Within any one of the three streams of Southern Comprehensive class differences are negligible; it is streaming which has the major impact upon the shaping of educational opportunity. Even in the selective secondary schools the influence of class is localized rather than general across the total sample. The bottom stream secondary modern school pupils are relatively undifferentiated by their class backgrounds; they are so clearly defined as failures by the educational system that not even a middle class family can

---

on the following criteria: (1) education: all those who desire some form of further education–high aspirations; all other responses – low aspirations; (2) Occupation: 'high status white collar'–high aspirations; 'low status white collar' and 'working manual'–low aspirations, all other replies have been excluded; (3) Politics: desire to perform a political role, regardless of type–high aspirations; all alternative choices–low aspirations.

[7] All the information on which these correlations are based is available in the previous chapter. If the reader wants to cross check the figures, he is reminded of the modifications, already referred to in this chapter, which were introduced before the tests were carried out.

counteract this. It is amongst the relatively privileged, especially the grammar school children, that class maintains its strongest hold. This is a perfect example of how the socialization agents crystallize to increase their impact: the middle class child enters the high status school and is still able to compete more successfully than his fellow pupil from a working class environment. This is a fairly good indication of the interests to which the grammar schools are most attuned.

The gap between secondary modern and grammar schools appears very large but in fact the differences are concentrated; it is the middle class youths who are most influenced by the type of secondary school they attend. The implication is that the child from a middle class family is much more likely to respond to educational failure than the working class boy is to react to educational sucess. If this is so then it appears to be harder to break down traditional working class norms than to create new patterns of behaviour for the middle class adolescents.

Streaming reinforces the contrasts associated with class and school; the influences overlap in such a way as to establish differential status positions. This is illustrated by the big division in educational aspirations between the top and bottom streams of working class adolescents in the secondary modern schools. As expected it is the top stream pupils who have the higher aspirations. Therefore, those at the bottom of the status hierarchy – the working class, bottom stream, secondary modern adolescents – have very different response patterns from even closely related social groups. It is these children, and their parents, who in Michael Young's terms probably find the school such an alien institution.

Occupational Aspirations

	Significant Differences	
	Tripartite Schools	*Southern Comprehensive*
Class	Not significant	Not significant
School	0·01	Not applicable
Streaming	0·01	0·01

For the comprehensive schools there is a strong similarity between educational and occupational patterns. Streaming is carefully defining future status positions but it must be remembered that placement in a stream is partially dependent upon class background. The influence of class is further diminished but it retains some hold upon the top stream grammar school pupils. This is in line with the notion of overlapping influence of the socialization agents. However, this works in opposite ways at the two ends of the continuum: the middle class, grammar school boy is able to maintain his advantage over the potentially mobile, working class boy, even if they are both in the top stream; but in the bottom streams of the secondary moderns all pupils, regardless of class background, select the low status jobs and have little desire for further education. There appears to be a line below which the child cannot fall and still expect his family to assist in maintaining, or improving, his social status.

As before, the big division between secondary modern and grammar schools is for the top stream, middle class adolescents. This reaffirms the special sensitivity of middle class children to their position in the educational structure. At the same time it is possible to argue that if these adolescents are highly realistic in their choice of future jobs, it is more in response to their location in the schooling hierarchy than initial family socialization.

Streaming patterns provide another perfect illustration of how the socialization influences can hold together. The statistically significant differences arise out of two subsamples: middle class grammar school, and working class secondary modern pupils.[8] Of course one indirect implication of this is that the secondary modern school effectively depresses the aspirations of all middle class children, regardless of stream placement. Occupational aspirations are very similar for top and bottom stream, middle class secondary modern adolescents, and at the same time there are big differences between the grammar and secondary modern pupils.

Political Roles

Significant Differences

	Tripartite Schools	*Southern Comprehensive*
Class	0·01	Not significant
School	Not significant	Not applicable
Streaming	Not significant	Not significant

Up to now there has been consistency across all the varying

[8] This is a comparison of the top and bottom stream, middle class, grammar school pupils, and the top and bottom stream, working class, secondary modern school pupils.

subsamples: the division between middle class and working class, grammar and secondary modern schools, top and bottom streams, has resulted in higher aspirations for the former groups. However the total chi square values for political aspirations conceal some important inconsistencies. In addition although the class differences in the selective schools are significant, this is true of only one sub-section – bottom stream secondary modern pupils. Generally speaking, therefore, there is a coalition of minimal variations and inconsistent trends.

If it is accepted that political aspirations should be treated as a special case, then the above information leads to a number of important observations. The original assumption that by the age of 15 the school takes over from class background as the most important determinant of behaviour has strong support. The evidence also suggests that the predicted overlap of class and school is a reality. These adolescents have been part of the educational system for about ten years. It has had plenty of time in which to establish itself at the focal point of their lives; confirming, supplementing or supplanting ways learnt in the family.

The overall picture of the relationship between class, school, streaming and status aspirations is illustrated by the following table:

Status Aspirations[9]

	The Tripartite Schools			Southern Comprehensive		
	Educ.	Jobs	Politics	Educ.	Jobs	Politics
Class	×		×			
School	×	×		N.A.	N.A.	N.A.
Streaming	×	×		×	×	

On the basis of this evidence it is fair to conclude that position in the schooling system is the most potent force in the formulation of educational and occupational aspirations for the largest number of individuals in the sample.[10] At the same time the impact of social

[9] An × indicates there are significant differences.

[10] Of course this is only in terms of the variables introduced in this study. Probably the most important excluded item is I.Q. which probably ties in closely with school and streaming differences. The whole issue is still wide open, for if I.Q. is primarily an hereditary characteristic then the family reclaims its dominant position, and yet there is evidence which suggests that school structure can, among other things, change I.Q. scores. For a more detailed analysis of the debate see above, pp. 14–16.

class is much more influential in the tripartite than the comprehensive schools. Southern Comprehensive is creating a true meritocracy rather than merely perpetuating class differences within a new framework.

The major social categories arise from harmonious interaction of the socialization agents: middle class adolescents in the top streams of the grammar schools, or working class pupils in the bottom streams of the secondary moderns. The previous chapter showed that there were the groups with the most differentiated status aspirations. As differences have now been measured in controlled situations, these extreme ends of the social continuum have not been compared. This illustrates the importance of keeping in mind the trends which emerge when the independent influences interact with one another. However, this attempt to assess the relative impact of the home and the school clarifies their relationship over time.

Not everyone experiences harmony in his social training; how this conflict is resolved provides a number of insights into the general functioning of society. Two good examples in this study are middle class adolescents in the bottom streams of the secondary moderns, and the working class pupils in the top streams of the grammar schools. The former adopt the norms of their working class school-friends, while the latter still have difficulty in competing with their middle class peers. The implication is that given a highly selective educational system, the stigma of failure is more potent than the badge of success; there are some barriers against falling down the slippery slope but plenty which prevent easy upward social mobility.

The evidence does suggest that it is possible to introduce social change by modifying the structure of the educational system. At the same time the direction of the present social change is rather ominous; it may help to solve the manpower shortages of the technological society but it is clearly not likely to create a more equitable class structure. Reservations surrounding the statistical procedures result in more tentative conclusions on the nature of the socialization process but at least they question the pre-eminent past position of the family by suggesting that it is increasingly more important to ascertain how the family relates to the school.[11]

[11] Besides not introducing sufficient socialization agents, another weakness is the paucity of measures for those which are a part of the study. Family is something more than a position in the class hierarchy just as schooling means more than school type or streaming.

7

POLITICAL SOCIALIZATION:
CONFORMISTS AND DEVIANTS

It is part of the conventional wisdom of political science that political party loyalties are transferred within the family. On the basis of evidence from his voting study Berelson states, '. . . about 75 per cent of the first voters in the community sided with their fathers in their political choice.'[1] This is confirmed by the recent British study of Butler and Stokes: 'But it is the direction on the child's partisanship that is the foremost legacy of the early years. A child is very likely to share his parents' party preference. Partisanship over the individual's lifetime has some of the quality of a photographic reproduction that deteriorates with time: it is a fairly sharp copy of the parents' original at the beginning of political awareness, but over the years it becomes somewhat blurred, although remaining easily recognizable.'[2]

It is widely accepted that change in the social status of children and parents can upset well founded family patterns of voting behaviour. To quote from Berelson again, '. . . the comparative social status of the son or the daughter is a qualifying factor to the father's political tradition.'[3] Most of the working class children at grammar school are in the process of obtaining higher status roles than their parents. An increasing awareness of this, as well as the pressure exerted by a middle class school environment, will act to undermine traditional family allegiances. This is assuming, of course, that this involves support for the Labour party which is not

[1] *op. cit.*, p. 95.
[2] David Butler and Donald Stokes, *Political Change in Britain*, London, Macmillan, 1969, p. 47.
[3] *op. cit.*, p. 102.

a foregone conclusion in view of their rather special working class family environment.[4] This is, therefore, another context in which to assess the interaction of family and school.

A second interest in party loyalties is trying to assess their implication for political behaviour. What does it mean to indicate support for one of the major parties? What are the consequences of not forming a party identification? The American voting studies which have been carried out by the University of Michigan regard party identification as one of the three social-psychological determinants of voting behaviour.[5] Identification implies something more than the mere willingness to vote for a particular political party at election time. As, over time, the individual establishes his party loyalty, he comes to believe that it represents a correct position on a number of political issues. There was a wide consensus between Democrats and Republicans as to what their respective parties were supposed to stand for. Party loyalties, therefore, should have a direct relationship to the second set of dependent variables—the attitudinal questions.

The Family and Political Affiliations

The two following hypotheses cover adolescent responses in opposing family situations:

H1 When parental party affiliations are uniform then the child will adopt the preference of his parents.

H2 When parental party affiliations are in conflict then the child will have no party preference.

In the first situation the individual is receiving uniform stimuli from his home environment: this should ensure that he adheres to parental loyalties. In the second case the adolescent is in a dilemma, for he receives inconsistent messages. He is most likely to resolve this by attempting to withdraw from the conflict by either not forming a party preference or possibly by establishing one not acceptable to the immediate family circle. The American voting studies incorpor-

---

[4] On this see above, pp. 66–8.

[5] Angus Campbell, Gerald Gurin and Warren E. Miller, *The Voter Decides*, Illinois, Row Peterson, 1954. The other two determinants are issue orientation and candidate choice. The conclusion is that in most elections, for the majority of the electorate, party identification is the single most important influence guiding the individual voter.

ate similar conflict situations into their research that in fact suggests the former outcome: 'That is to say, we expect that the greater the number of positive forces activating an individual in the election situation the more likely he will be to respond. When the forces acting on a person are in conflict, however, we expect that his response will be reduced.'[6]

TABLE I

Adolescent Party Loyalties—Parental Loyalties are Uniform

| | Adolescents | | | | |
	Conservative	Labour	Liberal	None[7]	Total
	%	%	%	%	Ns.
Parents					
Conservative	73	4	11	12	312
Labour	4	76	6	14	470
Liberal	17	9	55	20	77
None[7]	16	25	6	53	263

The trend suggested by the first hypothesis does exist. In view of the findings of both American and British studies centred on this aspect of political socialization it would have been more than surprising if it had not. There are, however, one or two fluctuations. There is considerable deviation from parents with uniform Liberal party affiliations, which probably reflects the minority position of the Liberal party. The influences to which this adolescent is exposed —peer groups are very relevant in this context—are likely to encourage the desertion of parental political traditions. There is also socialization into apparent political apathy but, as with Liberal party preferences, this is less likely to be transferred by the family than commitments to either of the two major parties.[8]

The information in Table 2 invalidates the second hypothesis; even in conflict situations there is still a strong tendency to select

[6] *ibid.*, p. 87.

[7] This is composed of a variety of responses: those who did not reply to the question, those who responded 'don't know', and those who rejected all party labels.

[8] There was some reluctance to reveal parental political affiliations and this may account for the trend; the parents are not politically apathetic so in reality the adolescents are following, rather than deviating from, family patterns.

TABLE 2

Adolescent Party Loyalties – Parental Loyalties Conflict

| | Adolescents | | | |
	Same party loyalty as parent(s)	Different party loyalty to parent(s)	None	Total
	%	%	%	Ns.
Parents[9]				
Postitive and uniform	73	14	13	872
Positive but conflict	72	14	14	149
One parent with, the other without a party preference	56	18	25	195

parties within the family orbit. Boys lean slightly towards their father's choice and there is an even more pronounced selection of the mother's party by the girls. However, in the working class families both boys and girls are more likely to select the mother's party. This ties in with the Bethnal Green findings on the dominant role of the mother in working class families.[10] There is almost certainly a sharing of many values between the working class families of Bethnal Green and Northern Conurbation.

The families in which there is one parent with a party preference and the other without, give rise to some interesting points. In the first place the adolescents are inclined to follow the lead of the parent who is politically aware, but there are also relatively high levels of both apathy and deviance. In fact both are higher within the framework of this family then where there is outright opposition between the two parents. It can only be surmised that we are starting to embrace those families in which politics is of low salience; there is not much overt political socialization on the part of either parent.

Social Class and Political Affiliations

The most emphasized aspect of party support in England is its class bias. The British voting studies show that the relationship

[9] 'Positive' simply means the parent(s) has a party label.
[10] Michael Young and Peter Willmott, *Family and Kinship in East London*, London, Routledge and Kegan Paul, 1957.

between social class and voting behaviour is as strong as the link between the political party affiliations of parents and children. In traditional terms the Labour party has been the champion of the working class man while the Conservative party has attracted most of its support from the middle class.[11] The way class and political affiliations interact gives rise to some of the most important cross-pressured groups. Keeping matters at a very simple level results in the following possible ties:

1. A middle class background and a Conservative party label
2. A working class   ,,   ,, ,, Labour party label
3. A middle class   ,,   ,, ,,   ,,   ,,   ,,
4. A working class   ,,   ,, ,, Conservative party label

The third and fourth groups are the cross-pressured adolescents. These individuals prefer political parties which traditionally have been identified with interests in opposition to their own social class position. There should be different responses to the attitudinal questions on the basis of both party identification and class background; we can expect differences between the middle and working class Labour party adolescents as well between the Labour and Conservative party adolescents in general.[12]

TABLE 3

Class and Adolescent Party Loyalties[13]

	Conservative	Labour	Liberal	None	Total
	%	%	%	%	Ns.
Upper middle	44	16	25	16	32
Middle class	46	24	19	12	221
Lower middle	34	28	15	23	384
Skilled working	18	51	9	22	499
Other working	19	45	7	29	326

The above distributions are very much as anticipated, but there is still a substantial minority of cross-pressured adolescents whose

[11] For a statement on the *decreasing* importance of class see Richard Rose, *People in Politics*, London, Faber and Faber, 1970, pp. 44–6.

[12] Naturally there should also be different response patterns for the middle and working class, Conservative party adolescents.

[13] A few individuals who indicated their support for a minority party, or split their allegiance, have been excluded from the table.

response to the attitudinal questions will be especially noted. On the five point class scale there is not a straightforward link between social class and major party affiliations. The strongest support for the Conservative party comes from the middle class youths and for the Labour party from adolescents whose fathers are skilled workers. Although the Liberal party has a much stronger appeal to the middle than the working class subsample, it scores particularly heavily amongst the upper middle class stratum. Liberal party adherents are more prevalent in this study than in the general adult population which is well illustrated by the fact that there is as much middle class support for the Liberal party as there are working class Tories.[14]

Both skilled and unskilled working class adolescents are inclined to have fewer established party affiliations than the middle class youths, including those from lower middle class families. However, this disguises the fact that the most important distinctions are between those adolescents from unskilled working class and middle class families; indeed the pattern for the skilled working and lower middle class strata are very similar. Again there is a close connection between these trends and those for the adult population.[15] Not only does political apathy—measured by the lack of a political party label—appear at a relatively early age but the individuals among whom it appears are also clearly defined. Even at this stage it is not hard to predict that this will be reinforced by schooling experiences.

Class, School and Political Affiliations

The potential impact of the grammar school upon the political affiliations of its working class pupils can be expressed concretely in the following hypothesis:

H3 Working class pupils at grammar school will tend to rebel against uniform parental Labour party identifications.

[14] 11·2 and 8·6 per cent of the adult population voted for the Liberal party in the General Elections of 1964 and 1966 respectively. Of course this is not a percentage of the total adult population but just of the actual voters amongst those registered to vote. In addition Liberal candidates did not stand in every constituency.

[15] Both the American and British voting studies show the concentration of the non-voters amongst the unskilled working class stratum. For a sophisticated analysis of the whole problem see, G. A. Almond and S. Verba, *The Civic Culture*, Princeton, The University Press, Chapter Six.

The middle class adolescent at the secondary modern school is in a very different psychological position from the working class, grammar school boy for socially he is potentially downwardly mobile. He may well perceive his probable future position in the society and cling to the family tradition of voting for the Conservative party—again assuming this actually exists—as a means of holding on to his status. Lipset's research suggests that many of the extreme right wing movements in the United States receive their strongest backing from individuals with status problems.[16] Admittedly the Conservative party is a long way from the extremist right wing political groups, but it is undoubtedly the party of tradition and order, which could be a sufficient reason to support it if the individual feels a status threat. The peer group cultures of the secondary modern schools are unlikely to induce favourable attitudes towards the Conservative party. Therefore, regardless of psychological pressures, the sociological forces place him in a conflict situation. The end result may well be the changing of loyalties or alternatively a failure to adopt a party label. These alternatives can be stated concisely in the form of two hypotheses:

H4 Adolescents who rebel against uniform parental Conservative party affiliations will tend to be middle class pupils at secondary modern schools.

H5 The strongest allegiance to the Conservative party will come from the middle class adolescents who attend secondary modern schools.

It is clear from Table 4 that the grammar school appears to have some impact on the political affiliations of its working class pupils. In fact it is the grammar school girls with Labour party parents who are most prone to change their allegiance. Women are more flexible regarding their party loyalties; married women, for example, are quite likely not to vote, or change their preference, to avoid conflicting with their husbands.[17] We have already seen that the girls are less likely to have formed a party identification; a picture, therefore, is emerging of their lower political awareness and more ready response to social pressure. As interest in politics is traditionally the prerogative of men, this is not too surprising.

[16] Seymour M. Lipset, 'The Sources of the Radical Right', in Daniel Bell (ed.), *The Radical Right*, New York, Doubleday, 1963, pp. 259–312.

[17] On this see Lazarsfeld, *op. cit.*, p. 141, and Robert E. Lane, *Political Life*, Chicago, The Free Press, 1959, pp. 209–11.

TABLE 4

Class, School and Party Loyalties

	Conservative	Labour	Liberal	Other	None	Total
	%	%	%	%	%	Ns.
Both parents Labour and working class						
Grammar school	4	59	17	7	14	29
Secondary modern	3	78	3	0	16	165
Both parents Conservative and middle class						
Grammar school	72	4	16	0	9	129
Secondary modern	83	3	8	0	6	36

Clearly the information in Table 4 invalidates the fourth hypothesis, but at the same time it provides only limited support for the fifth hypothesis. Nonetheless it does suggest that different psychological and social mechanisms operate for those likely to move upwards or downwards in society.[18] Further evidence reveals that there is middle class rejection of the Labour party by both grammar and secondary modern pupils, as well as working class rejection of the Conservative party, again by both grammar and secondary modern pupils. However because of the well established links between class, school and party, most middle class rebellion against the Conservative party is within the context of the grammar school, and working class antipathy to established Labour party allegiances within the framework of the secondary modern schools.

Most of the middle class adolescents who have Labour party allegiances are at grammar schools while most of the Conservative, working class youths attend secondary moderns. At the same time both groups are generally reflecting the preferences of their parents. The school, therefore, does not upset loyalty patterns for most of the adolescents. It is reasonable to conclude that where there is cross-pressuring between class and political affiliations it is a reflection of family patterns which naturally existed long before entry into the secondary schools.[19]

[18] As Maccoby states: 'It appears, then, that those who move up the social scale seek to identify themselves with the political values of the higher group, but those who move down cling to the symbols of their former status.' See E. Maccoby, 'Youth and Political Change', *Public Opinion Quarterly*, Volume 18, 1954, p. 35.

[19] As stated in the previous paragraph the ties between class and school

Political Apathy

If the individual has a party label he will in all likelihood go on to work within the mainstream of the political process: political activity, even if it implies the mere recording of a vote at election time, will have some meaning for him. As most of the sample are 14-year-olds it is reasonable to expect some of them to have doubts about their future party allegiance. Perhaps within itself this is an adequate explanation of those responses which show uncertainty but it is less adequate where there is a straight rejection of all the parties.[20] The main point of interest is to examine the social forces which are associated with political apathy; to see if there are contrasting flows through the system which lead to radically different levels of political awareness.

TABLE 5

Class, School and Adolescent Party Loyalties—the Tripartite Schools

	Party preference	None	Total
	%	%	Ns.
Super Grammar			
Middle class	90	10	145
Working class	81	19	16
Suburban Girls' Grammar			
Middle class	91	9	43
Working class	(7)	(0)	(7)
LEA grammar schools			
1st stream			
Middle class	76	24	55
Working class	85	15	20
2nd stream			
Middle class	93	7	15
Working class	(7)	(1)	(8)

ensure that most middle class Labour party allegiants are at grammar school, while most working class Conservatives attend secondary moderns. They are following, for the most part, a family pattern and only a few of them deviate from it.

[20] This is the distinction between those who 'don't know' what party appeals to them and those who reject the likelihood of ever supporting a political party.

TABLE 5–*continued*

	Party preference	None	Total
	%	%	Ns.
3rd stream			
Middle class	80	20	46
Working class	78	22	18
Secondary modern schools			
1st stream			
Middle class	81	19	75
Working class	80	20	169
2nd stream			
Middle class	88	13	16
Working class	77	23	100
3rd stream			
Middle class	75	25	24
Working class	68	32	151
Home County Bilateral			
1st stream			
Middle class	91	9	34
Working class	77	23	13
2nd stream			
Middle class	75	25	12
Working class	(7)	(1)	(8)
3rd stream	(2)	(3)	(5)
Middle class			
Working class	79	21	34

Although the distinctions are not especially large, nevertheless there is a slight trend in the expected direction. The highest concentration of political apathy is in the bottom streams of the secondary modern schools, but even in this case positive identifications are surprisingly high–nearly 70 per cent for the working class adolescents. Over this particular period the major political parties had widespread support throughout the population.[21] Given the previous

[21] The opinion polls for the adult population show that allegiances to the major parties fluctuate over time and there is evidence to suggest that much the same is true of adolescents. However there are indications that many young people are permanently rejecting the accepted party labels and

links between the selective and comprehensive schools there is no reason to suspect that they will differ on this issue.

TABLE 6

Class, School and Adolescent Political Loyalties – the Comprehensive Schools

	Party preference	None	Total
	%	%	Ns.
Southern Comprehensive			
1st stream			
Middle class	78	22	36
Working class	56	44	18
2nd stream			
Middle class	69	31	91
Working class	67	33	97
3rd stream			
Middle class	67	33	15
Working class	63	37	49
Northern Comprehensive			
1st stream			
Middle class	79	21	24
Working class	85	15	67
2nd stream			
Middle class	(4)	(1)	(5)
Working class	89	11	47
3rd stream			
Middle class	(2)	(1)	(3)
Working class	88	13	16

Once again the percentage of party identifiers is uniformly high. The one exception is the working class youths in the top stream of Southern Comprehensives. They are nearly all rejecting uniform parental, Labour party affiliations, and instead of outright rebellion they fail to record a party preference.[22] In some ways they are in a

becoming increasingly politically apathetic. On this see R. A. Butler, *English Secondary School Adolescents: An Analysis of Political Discontent*, unpublished M.A. Thesis, The University of Sussex, 1969.

[22] Outright rebellion would be expressed by moving over to either the Conservative or Liberal party.

similar social situation to the working class youths at grammar schools and it is significant that the responses follow more or less the same line. This is one indication of the social conflict which exists within the comprehensive school; the school appears to be changing the behaviour of working class youths in a number of dimensions. Similar reasoning is one possible explanation of the rather unusual patterns which emerge at Northern Comprehensive. In this school the most isolated individual is the middle class child whose parents vote for the Conservative party, and this is the very group which shows the least solidarity; as before the adolescents incline towards apathy rather than outright rebellion.[23] The exact implications, therefore, of the lack of a party label may vary from both school to school and stream to stream. For example in the top streams of the secondary moderns the adolescents without party preferences come in the main from families in which this is the norm; in the bottom streams there is the rejection of uniform parental affiliations, nearly all favouring the Labour party. In one case there is the continuation of family patterns while in the other there is an apparent increase in political apathy.

The evidence presented in this chapter confirms that most young people acquire their party allegiances within the family. At the same time, social mobility strains traditional family patterns; it is the working class, grammar school girls who are most likely to reject the Labour party identification of their parents. The Conservative party appears to represent a definite status hold for the middle class adolescents at secondary modern schools; a way of distinguishing themselves from their peers. Although the level of positive party identifications is generally high, there is still a tendency for political apathy to be related to a well defined syndrome of social forces; working class pupils in the bottom streams of the secondary modern schools follow a path which matches their lower role aspirations.

[23] The sparsity of numbers suggests that this conclusion should be treated cautiously. In general the comprehensive schools do not appear to disturb the political patterns of either their working class or middle class pupils. At Northern Comprehensive the overwhelming working class composition appears to ensure Labour party solidarity. At Southern Comprehensive, class and party distributions are relatively even; *no one group dominates to facilitate the resocialization of minority subsamples.*

8

DEVELOPING ATTITUDES

Each of the attitudinal questions considers an important aspect of the organization of English society. The first question asks the adolescent for his opinion of the 11+ examination; more specifically whether it should be retained or abolished.[1] The 11+ is at the very foundation of the post 1944 secondary educational system. For the past twenty-five years it has been the dominating feature in the school lives of most children. Probably it has been subjected to more emotional outpouring than any other single facet of the educational structure, as well as the object of a considerable amount of very serious research. Feelings, both for and against, run high, with not all the professional educationalists on one side of the fence.[2] The second question examines the child's perception of the world of work which many of them are on the verge of entering; they are asked for some assessment of the criteria which determine the chances of finding a good job.[3] Most of adult life is spent at work and from the society's point of view it is desirable that the adolescent should feel that when he finally enters the job market the conditions which govern his placement and promotion are equitable. The third question analyses adolescent conceptions of the relationship between government and people.[4] It is one of the planks of parliamentary democracy that the political élite, especially those who form the government of the day, are ultimately responsible to the people. The origins of political

---

[1] See the Appendix, question 25.

[2] For a brief discussion of the debate see above, pp. 14–16. It is more accurate to say that the 11 + is generally out of favour rather than that the principle of non-selection is universally accepted.

[3] See the Appendix, question 34.

[4] See the Appendix, question 54.

apathy have already been outlined; this will provide some guide to the growth of political cynicism. Britain is often considered to be a society rigidly divided along class lines. The final question considers the adolescents' opinion on this issue: Does the schoolboy feel that opportunities in this society are closely curtailed by the class structure?[5]

In theory there is a close relationship between the four questions: a rigidity in class relations may simply mean the restricting of educational and job opportunities, or alternatively an unfair educational system probably leads to the perpetuation of the same bias in the competition for jobs. If the adolescents see such links then there should be similar distributions for each of the questions.

The four issues will not have the same relevance for all the adolescents in the study which is best illustrated by the 11 + question. The education the adolescents are receiving is closely tied up with their performance in this examination. If they realize that this link does exist, then each school will have a rather distinctive influence upon attitudes. Furthermore the campaign against the 11 + has often been interpreted as a threat against the grammar schools; the fact that in a comprehensive scheme the secondary moderns will also disappear is generally overlooked. If the grammar school pupil sees the abolition of the selective examinations as a threat to his educational progress then he should come out in favour of its retention. Similar pressures act upon the comprehensive school adolescent but in an opposite direction; he is part of the new system arising out of the ashes of the old, discredited order. If all is well he presumably has a very real interest in attacking the old order and defending the new.

The questions have been structured to allow the following range of responses:

1. Very satisfied with the status quo   SATISFIED
2. Satisfied with the status quo   RESPONSES

3. Dissatisfied with the status quo   DISSATISFIED
4. Very dissatisfied with the status quo   RESPONSES

5. No opinion on the issue   WITHDRAWAL
6. Don't know what to think   RESPONSES

[5] See the Appendix, question 62.

There are, therefore, two different types of positive responses, replies 1, 2, 3, and 4; and one withdrawal response, replies 5 and 6. In presenting the evidence, the most frequent comparisons will be made between positive and withdrawal responses or satisfied and dissatisfied responses.

The positive and withdrawal responses are possible indications of levels of system involvement: there are various intensities of interest in the organization of this society. At the same time it is possible to view this distribution as a measure of deferential attitudes; a withdrawal response implying either that the individual either lacks the capacity to take a definite stand or he is not the person generally called upon to answer, or supposedly interested in answering, such questions.[6] The satisfied and dissatisfied responses are aimed at determining the pro- and anti-system groups. It must be remembered that satisfaction or dissatisfaction is expressed in terms of only specific aspects of the structure or values of this society; it is possible, but not likely, that the individual who expresses hostility to the *status quo* on all four questions still retains his faith in the overall organization of the system.

If, as was maintained in the previous chapter, the different party labels represent contrasting ideological positions, then they will affect the direction of the responses to these questions. In the past the split between the Conservative and Labour parties has undoubtedly been more pronounced than the division between the Republican and Democratic parties. Party identifications, therefore, should be more clearly defined in Britain than in the United States. Burke probably still sums up better than anyone else the ethos of the Conservative party: deep respect for the structure of society with changes introduced only after careful deliberation and then only slowly with full respect being given to past institutions and traditions.[7] One important impetus for the creation of the Labour party was the desire to provide British society with a more equitable structure; it had to change to ensure that a larger percentage of the people

[6] It is never easy to interpret responses. The alternatives offered are very clear and the replies have to be taken at face value. The 'don't know' replies cause most problems: it may represent a genuine confusion rather than a lack of interest in the issue at stake. The important point is that each type of response should be seen as quite distinctive entities and here there is no real problem.

[7] Edmund Burke, *Reflections on the Revolution in France*, London, Dent and Son, 1910.

received greater rewards, rewards which they had earned and were consequently theirs by right. These stereotypes may be removed somewhat from present day realities but they probably still provide the basic distinction in party identifications. The Labour party adolescents should, therefore, turn out to be opposed to the present structure of society and the Conservatives to favour it. Of course if this is indeed the age of the politics of consensus then there should be a large number of common responses. The Liberals are an intriguing problem. For a long time they have been eclipsed in the national scene. Although in the last few years this has changed somewhat, they very rarely steal the limelight. What does it mean, therefore, to be a supporter of the Liberal party? It is safe to predict a higher percentage of withdrawal responses and more divergence between the two types of positive responses than for the adolescents with major party preferences.

The positive and withdrawal responses require a comparison of the trends for adolescents with and without established party preferences. Withdrawal responses should not only correlate highly with those without party attachments but also with those who occupy inferior positions in the class and school hierarchies.

It is possible for the influence of class to take a number of different directions. Withdrawal responses should increase in moving through the class scale, from the upper middle class to the adolescents from unskilled working class families. This accepts the plausibility of some of the customary views of working class behaviour; that there is a tendency to be less articulate and more deferential than the middle classes. Deference, however, may result in satisfaction with the system, belief that this is indeed the good society. As the middle class child receives more rewards from the society this should go hand in hand with favourable dispositions towards it. However, scarce resources also restrict middle class ambitions; the difficulty of obtaining a university place is a good illustration of this point. The end result could be hostility to the educational system in general.

The inferior status of the secondary modern schools could lead to intense hostility on the part of their pupils with the *status quo*. However, inferiority may breed indifference; but if deference springs from assumed ignorance then these may well be the very adolescents who are most satisfied with the present organization of society. Limited facilities also affect grammar school adolescents: not all of them sit the G.C.E. examinations, let alone go on to read for a degree at university. What reaction follows from a failure to gain these fairly widely distributed rewards?[8]

The comprehensive school pupils are in a very delicate situation. Streaming reintroduces many of the old rigidities and divisions which exist in the tripartite secondary schools. They may realize this and over-react against the knowledge that the new community is little better than the old. Of course this depends partially on their position in the comprehensive school and whether they have any idea that they are supposedly part of a new system. School may be simply school no matter what label it is given. The 11 + question should be a very sensitive measure of these adolescents' attitudes.

Clearly it is much more difficult to predict the probable responses for attitudes than aspirations; the potential for divergent influences is so much greater for all the variables. However the problems may decrease somewhat when the various influences are interrelated, for this establishes more clearcut differences between the categories: the upper middle class, direct grant grammar school adolescents with established party loyalties on the one hand, and the secondary modern school children from unskilled working class families without the remotest interest in politics on the other hand. There has been a great deal of research into status aspirations and little on the development of attitudes so the hypotheses will still be more tentative than in previous chapters.

Positive—Withdrawal Responses
The tripartite schools

The responses in Table 1 follow a fairly well defined pattern: withdrawal replies are closely associated with the working class, secondary modern adolescents who have no definite party loyalties, while positive replies correlate highly with exactly the reverse set of social forces. Although the differences are very much as predicted, they are not as great as for the aspirational data; in grammar schools, for example, the class gap is barely in the expected direction.

Each question results in somewhat distinctive distributions. The 11 + question has the highest percentage of positive replies. The

---

[8] Although not within the grasp of the overwhelming majority of adolescents, they are well known to the grammar schoolchildren.

examination is common to the experience of nearly everyone in the sample and so it is not surprising it should receive this high level of positive replies. Most working class youths are quite capable of giving a positive answer to the question on job selection. They are much more likely to be out at work at an earlier age than middle class children; particularly as so many of them are at secondary modern schools. There is pressure, therefore, to quickly come to terms with the occupational structure. It is significant, that in relation to the other questions, most withdrawal responses on this item come from the upper middle class boys at Super Grammar, the very persons whose job choice will be delayed for at least a few years.[9]

The political question has evoked the largest number of withdrawal responses. The link between apathy over party labels, and apparent indifference to this issue, is strong; at a relatively early age there are a well-defined minority of adolescents who appear to be opting out of all political commitments.[10]

TABLE I

Class, School and Political Affiliations: Attitudes in the Tripartite Schools

| | Education[11] | | Jobs[11] | | Politics[11] | | Class[11] | | |
	Pos.	With.	Pos.	With.	Pos.	With.	Pos.	With.	Total
	%	%	%	%	%	%	%	%	Ns.
Direct Grant									
Middle class									
Party									
label	94	6	79	21	84	16	89	11	131
No party	79	21	71	29	57	43	86	14	14
Working class									
Party									
label	85	15	54	46	85	15	69	31	13
No party	(3)	(0)	(3)	(0)	(2)	(1)	(2)	(1)	(3)

[9] They may already have a job in mind but it is unlikely to be the pressing issue faced by the 15-year-old school leavers.

[10] The group is defined by its concentration in the bottom streams of the secondary modern schools, in particular their working class pupils.

[11] These headings refer to the four attitudinal questions; it should be evident from the labels alone which questions they refer to.

TABLE I—*continued*

LEA Grammar
Middle class

Party label								
label	92	8	82	18	88	12	80	20	132
No party	93	7	78	22	81	19	70	30	27

Working class

Party label								
label	91	9	82	18	78	22	87	13	45
No party	(6)	(2)	(7)	(1)	(6)	(2)	(8)	(0)	(8)

Secondary Modern
Middle class

Party label								
label	80	20	75	25	77	23	70	30	93
No party	82	18	68	32	59	41	64	36	22

Working class

Party label								
label	79	21	66	34	61	39	58	42	315
No party	61	39	59	41	40	60	48	52	105

Bilateral
Middle class

Party label								
label	95	5	67	33	93	7	79	21	42
No party	(8)	(1)	(3)	(6)	(7)	(2)	(5)	(4)	(9)

Working class

Party label								
label	75	25	61	39	66	34	50	50	44
No party	82	18	82	18	82	18	55	45	11

It is possible to draw parallels between the pattern of Table 2 and the distribution of aspirations in the comprehensives. Southern Comprehensive maintains its relatively distinctive three tier hierarchy with a much higher percentage of withdrawal responses in the third stream than in any of the other schools.[12] There is not much of a distinction between top and second stream distributions, which leaves these lower stream adolescents in an even more isolated position than was the case for aspirations. As before, the streaming

[12] This includes the secondary modern schools but the numbers are rather sparse to allow good comparisons.

differences in Northern Comprehensive are not so clear cut. The shortage of numbers makes it more difficult to distinguish trends; there is a gentle increase in withdrawal responses from the first to the third streams with if anything a repetition of the uniqueness of the top stream pupils.

TABLE 2

Class, School and Political Affiliations:
Attitudes in the Comprehensive Schools

	Education		Jobs		Politics		Class		Total
	Pos.	With.	Pos.	With.	Pos.	With.	Pos.	With.	
	%	%	%	%	%	%	%	%	Ns.
Southern Comprehensive									
1st stream									
Middle class									
Party									
label	93	7	79	21	89	11	79	21	28
No party	(6)	(2)	(4)	(4)	(7)	(1)	(6)	(2)	(8)
Working class									
Party									
label	90	10	80	20	90	10	100	0	10
No party	(7)	(1)	(4)	(4)	(7)	(1)	(6)	(2)	(8)
2nd stream									
Middle class									
Party									
label	72	28	84	16	86	14	25	25	63
No party	61	39	61	39	50	50	61	39	28
Working class									
Party									
label	72	28	80	20	75	25	76	24	65
No party	56	44	69	31	37	63	66	34	32
3rd stream									
Middle class									
Party									
label	70	30	40	60	70	30	60	40	10
No party	(3)	(2)	(1)	(4)	(2)	(3)	(4)	(1)	(5)
Working class									
Party									
label	61	39	48	52	52	48	55	45	31
No party	56	44	56	44	44	56	33	67	18

TABLE 2—*continued*

Northern Comprehensive
1st stream
Middle class

Party								
label	89	11	84	16	79	21	100	0	19
No party	(5)	(0)	(5)	(0)	(3)	(2)	(5)	(0)	(5)

Working class

Party								
label	86	14	75	25	70	30	81	19	57
No party	90	10	80	20	80	20	60	40	10

2nd stream
Middle class

Party								
label	(2)	(2)	(2)	(2)	(3)	(1)	(4)	(0)	(4)
No party	(1)	(0)	(1)	(0)	(1)	(0)	(0)	(1)	(1)

Working class

Party								
label	90	10	74	26	81	19	60	40	42
No party	(5)	(0)	(4)	(1)	(3)	(2)	(4)	(1)	(5)

3rd stream
Middle class

Party								
label	(1)	(1)	(0)	(2)	(1)	(1)	(1)	(1)	(2)
No party	(0)	(1)	(1)	(0)	(0)	(1)	(0)	(1)	(1)

Working class

Party								
label	79	21	64	36	57	43	50	50	14
No party	(1)	(1)	(0)	(2)	(1)	(1)	(1)	(1)	(2)

Class and political affiliations act in the expected manner: fewer positive responses from the working class youths without party preferences. However the class contrasts within any one stream are not very pronounced which emphasizes the special position of the bottom stream pupils. Certainly the comprehensive schools are bringing about changes but the overall impression is that many diverse barriers to both social mobility and participation are being brought together and compounded into a rigid streaming hierarchy.

TABLE 3

Class, School and Political Affiliations: The Pattern of Positive Responses in the Tripartite Schools

	Education			Jobs			Politics			Class			Total
	Sat. %	Dis. %	With. %	Sat. %	Dis. %	With. %	Sat. %	Dis. %	With. %	Sat. %	Dis. %	With. %	Ns.
Direct Grant/LEA Grammar[13]													
Middle class													
Labour	28	63	9	32	49	18	62	28	11	20	71	9	65
Conservative	45	48	7	37	45	19	50	36	13	49	34	17	128
Liberal	31	61	7	24	54	21	21	59	20	26	57	17	70
Working class													
Labour	22	61	17	35	52	13	48	30	22	17	78	4	23
Conservative	56	31	13	25	50	25	19	50	31	25	56	19	76
Liberal	27	73	0	47	20	33	40	47	13	7	67	27	15
Secondary Modern													
Middle class													
Labour	18	65	18	38	35	26	41	41	18	32	35	32	34
Conservative	19	62	19	40	38	21	28	45	28	26	47	28	47

Working class													
Labour	24	53	23	37	28	35	29	27	44	12	42	46	197
Conservative	17	69	14	30	42	28	31	40	29	13	48	39	90
Liberal	15	62	23	23	27	50	19	39	42	19	50	31	26
Bilateral[14]													
Middle class													
Labour	45	55	0	27	27	45	82	18	0	45	36	18	11
Conservative	9	82	9	36	32	32	45	45	9	18	64	18	22
Working class													
Labour	14	59	28	34	24	41	38	28	34	10	34	55	29
Conservative	10	80	10	10	70	20	50	20	30	30	30	40	10

[13] Smallness of the working class categories compels the combining of Super Grammar and the L.E.A. controlled grammar schools. Any important difference will be noted in the text.

[14] There are hardly any middle or working class adolescents with Liberal party labels so they have been excluded.

Satisfied—Dissatisfied Responses
The tripartite schools

The satisfied/dissatisfied dimension (see Table 3) is altogether more complex than the positive/withdrawal pattern of responses. Class is not associated with a distinctive pro- or anti-system trend as the class scale is ascended, from unskilled working class to upper middle class, so both satisfied and dissatisfied responses increase and withdrawal responses decrease. Furthermore, regardless of the particular social class under observation, anti-system attitudes outweigh, usually to a considerable extent, pro-system responses. The only consistent direction for political party affiliations is that the Labour party adolescents are more convinced than the Conservatives of the responsibility of the government to the people. It is likely, in spite of explicit instructions to the contrary, that partisan political considerations influenced answers to this question. Because the political system is so intimately related to the party structures this may have been inevitable. To confirm this, the question should be put to the adolescents just after the defeat of the Labour party in a General Election.[15] The implication is that present divisions would be reversed; in other words the adolescent interprets the structure as satisfactory as long as the party he likes is winning. The contrasts are not so sharp among the grammar school pupils; presumably they have a greater knowledge of how the system works, or at least how it is supposed to work.

The assumptions about the nature of a Liberal party identification are not borne out. In nearly every case the Liberals are most hostile to the *status quo*. This is one indication that, although the party has suffered repeated electoral setbacks, they have been successful at building some form of recognizable party identity. The Liberals are also very sceptical about the responsibility of the government. Perhaps in view of constant Liberal pressure for parliamentary reform this could have been anticipated, assuming of course that the message was spreading this wide. Finally they are least likely to register withdrawal responses. The general image, therefore, is rather flattering: the Liberal adolescent is both involved in the society and committed to reform it.

---

[15] The information was collected shortly after the 1964 defeat of the Conservative party.

Even the school appears to have a local rather than a general impact, but it is still associated with more definite trends than the other socialization agents. The distributions for the 11+ question are the most distinctive: most hostility to the examination comes from those who have failed it but even the majority of grammar school adolescents are opposed to its continuation, at least in its present form. Stevens points out that the grammar school pupil is satisfied with the education he receives, and there is no evidence here to contradict this, but he is far from happy with the means by which he is selected for this education.

Super Grammar contains the pupils who are most satisfied with the *status quo*; their responses contrast quite noticeably even with the youths at the L.E.A. grammar schools. They record not only the highest percentage of satisfied responses but also the lowest number of dissatisfied replies. The middle class boy at this school, almost certainly a fee payer, comes from an especially privileged section of the community; the working class scholarship boy is on the verge of breaking into the Establishment. Both, therefore, have a very real stake in the present system. The same pressures exist for the other grammar school children but not with the same intensity.

For direct grant grammar school adolescents high role aspirations are accompanied by a strong pattern of pro-system attitudes. In his study of the University of Manchester undergraduates Richard Rose shows that the student's confidence about his own personal future is associated with deep antagonism towards the present structure of society.[16] The implications of this evidence, and of current events at many universities, is that these schoolboys will undergo a radical transformation. The university, because it cuts the adolescent loose from family and local ties, should encourage an increase in anti-system attitudes. Of course there are many ways of expressing opinions and even when action matches words it may be little more than the swansong before enslavement by the bureaucratic society.

The comprehensive schools

The main interest here is in whether streaming continues to provide the most important differences.

[16] Richard Rose, *Students in Society*, Manchester, University of Manchester Union, 1963.

TABLE 4

Class, School and Political Affiliations: The Pattern of Positive Responses in the Comprehensive Schools

	Education			Jobs			Politics			Class			Total
	Sat. %	Dis. %	With. %	Sat. %	Dis. %	With. %	Sat. %	Dis. %	With. %	Sat. %	Dis. %	With. %	Ns.
Southern Comprehensive[17]													
1st stream													
Middle class													
Labour	(0)	(9)	(0)	(3)	(4)	(2)	(5)	(4)	(0)	(4)	(3)	(2)	(9)
Conservative	21	64	14	29	50	21	57	21	21	50	29	21	14
Working class													
Labour	(0)	(3)	(1)	(3)	(1)	(0)	(2)	(2)	(0)	(0)	(4)	(0)	(4)
Conservative	(0)	(2)	(0)	(0)	(1)	(1)	(1)	(1)	(0)	(2)	(0)	(0)	(2)
2nd stream													
Middle class													
Labour	11	59	30	30	44	26	48	30	22	22	37	41	27
Conservative	0	72	28	52	36	12	44	44	12	36	48	16	25
Working class													
Labour	20	53	27	37	44	20	53	37	10	22	51	27	45
Conservative	9	73	18	36	45	18	27	27	55	9	73	18	11
3rd stream													
Middle class													
Labour	(2)	(3)	(1)	(1)	(2)	(3)	(2)	(2)	(2)	(2)	(2)	(2)	(6)
Conservative													

Working class													
Labour	25	25	50	30	20	50	45	5	50	20	40	40	20
Conservative	(0)	(5)	(1)	(0)	(3)	(3)	(1)	(1)	(4)	(1)	(2)	(3)	(6)
Northern Comprehensive[17]													
1st stream													
Middle class													
Labour	(2)	(5)	(1)	(5)	(1)	(2)	(5)	(1)	(2)	(5)	(3)	(0)	(8)
Conservative	(0)	(4)	(1)	(1)	(3)	(1)	(4)	(1)	(0)	(4)	(1)	(0)	(5)
Working class													
Labour	11	73	16	25	55	20	39	30	32	30	55	16	44
Conservative	(3)	(5)	(1)	(4)	(3)	(2)	(3)	(3)	(3)	(3)	(3)	(3)	(9)
2nd stream													
Middle class													
Labour	(0)	(1)	(2)	(1)	(1)	(1)	(1)	(1)	(1)	(1)	(2)	(0)	(3)
Working class													
Labour	21	65	14	25	54	21	50	32	18	11	39	50	28
Conservative	(0)	(4)	(0)	(1)	(2)	(1)	(3)	(0)	(1)	(0)	(2)	(2)	(4)
3rd stream													
Middle class													
Labour	(1)	(0)	(1)	(1)	(0)	(2)	(0)	(1)	(1)	(0)	(1)	(1)	(2)
Working class													
Labour	17	58	25	8	50	42	42	8	50	17	25	58	12
Conservative	(0)	(2)	(0)	(0)	(2)	(0)	(1)	(1)	(0)	(0)	(2)	(0)	(2)

[17] The Liberals have been excluded because of the shortage of numbers. There are no middle class Conservatives in either the second or third streams of Northern Comprehensive. Clearly the sparsity of numbers make any interpretations of this table very tentative.

82599

Still the majority of adolescents expressing an opinion are disillusioned with the present *status quo*. The fact that both satisfied and dissatisfied replies increase in number from the third to the first stream prevents clearcut differences.[18] There are one or two exceptions to this broad statement. Most hostility to the 11 + examination is expressed by the first and second stream pupils and at the same time they are no more likely to approve of the examination than the bottom stream adolescents.[19] The very individuals who should supposedly most benefit from the abolition of selection are either not prepared to express an opinion, one way or the other, or are as likely to favour its perpetuation as those who are least affected by changes in the educational system.

In the comprehensives there is less division between the Labour and Conservative party youths and this also applies to the political question. It is the top streams, at both comprehensive schools, which are most inclined to see the government as responsible to the people. This ties in with the greater impartiality of the grammar school adolescents on this particular issue.

Most American research emphasizes the high level of support there is for the political system. The earlier studies concentrated upon the President: his favourable image and the part the office plays in organizing political orientations.[20] More recently there has been some recognition that this earlier research was culture bound; it tended to make general conclusions on the basis of white, middle class samples.[21] The wide ranging response patterns of the varying groups within this sample support this criticism. Overall system support is far lower than in the American studies but it still varies from one group to the next.

Harry Eckstein has created a theory of stable democracy which takes England as the basic model.[22] Stable democracy is supported

[18] Introducing controls—for either class or political affiliation—does not affect this.

[19] The percentage of satisfied responses is very similar for all three streams. This is true for both the comprehensive schools.

[20] The amount of material available is quite enormous and the bibliography provides a reasonable selection of the most pertinent articles and books. As good a starting point as any is Fred I. Greenstein's work.

[21] For a good illustration of this point see, D. Jaros et al., 'The Malevolent Leaders: Political Socialization in an American Subculture', *American Political Science Review*, Volume 62, 1968, pp. 564–75.

[22] Harry Eckstein, *A Theory of Stable Democracy*, Princeton University Press, 1961.

by congruent authority patterns but there have to be some dispari-
ties: '. . . it follows that governmental democracy will tend to be
stable only if it is to a significant extent impure—if, in short, the
governmental authority pattern contains a balance of disparate
elements, of which democracy is an important part (but only a
part).'[23] Berelson advocates a somewhat different form of impurity,
'Thus the democratic citizen is called upon to pursue contradictory
goals: he must be active, yet passive; involved, yet not too involved;
influential, yet deferential.'[24] Almond and Verba conclude their five-
nation study with much the same argument: the civic culture is
partially dependent upon certain virtues within its citizenry; there
is need of a participation norm but it must be matched by a relatively low level of actual participation; activity is balanced by
cycles of involvement; orientation to the political system combines
affective and instrumental values; and finally within society there
must be both consensus and cleavage.[25] The starting point of these
studies is that democratic societies are under observation, whether
it be the United States or England, and yet traditional democratic
theory, which stressed certain characteristics of the individual
citizen, does not stand the test of empirical research work. The new
emphasis must be upon the character of the citizenry as a whole
rather than mere individuals. Of course there is some confusion as
to whether the split personality of the total population is also matched
by the split personality of the individual. As far as England is concerned the evidence of this study suggests that many persons are
systematically excluded from becoming effective members of the
community: they come from unfavoured family backgrounds, have
the most unenviable position in the fairly rigid educational hierarchy,
their role aspirations are generally speaking lower than all other
categories, and there is minimal interest in the structure of this
society including its political organization. It is rather pointless to
think of balanced involvement or cycles of involvement; all the
indications suggest that their level of participation is never likely to
be very high. They are Berelson's stability inducing, apathetic mass.[26]
It is difficult to describe the society as democratic when its very
structure assists the perpetuation of this group. Perhaps traditional
democratic theory makes certain idealistic demands which it is

[23] *ibid.*, p. 29.   [24] *op. cit.*, pp. 478–9.   [25] *op. cit.*, Chapter 15.
[26] This is part of the theme of his famous, or should it be infamous,
Chapter 14 in *Voting*.

impossible for many citizens to meet but at least they are worthwhile goals for any society to aim at.

Empirical theory is rarely little more than an elaborate defence of the *status quo*.[27] Furthermore this study throws some doubts on certain of the fundamental assumptions. Not even the potentially participant adolescents are very enamoured by the structure of English society. In the eyes of many school children this is a highly unsatisfactory way to run a society: jobs are distributed on unfair grounds and many good jobs are obtained through family connections; political leaders do not care about the electorate—once they have gained office they act like an isolated oligarchy; class relations are still too rigid—there are still great inequalities of wealth and although some people are privileged the vast majority are held back; and finally the 11+ examination is vindictive—it prevents many talented people from receiving a good education.[28]

The Crosspressured

There are a number of different forms of crosspressuring to consider. In the first place there is the interaction between class and political affiliations. Given the well established links between class and school, most of the working class Tories should attend the secondary moderns and the majority of middle class adolescents with Labour party loyalties the grammar schools. However, other alternatives are perfectly feasible and logically four crosspressured groups can be constructed:

1. Middle class, grammar school pupils with Labour party affiliations.
2. Middle class, secondary modern pupils with Conservative party affiliations.
3. Working class Tories who attend the grammar schools.
4. Working class Tories who attend secondary modern schools.

One would expect these adolescents to overidentify with their party

[27] A good example of an empirical theory of democracy that illustrates the point is Robert A. Dahl, *A Preface to Democratic Theory*, Chicago, The University Press, 1956.

[28] For a very different picture of young people see F. Musgrove, *Youth and the Social Order*, London, Routledge, 1964, and his *Family, Education and Society*, London, Routledge, 1966.

labels; in other words that most opposition to the *status quo* would come from the middle class ranks of the Labour party, and most support for it from the working class Tories. These statements should be treated very cautiously; the middle class Tories have both class position and party label suggesting favourable dispositions which can be greatly strengthened by a grammar school education.

The evidence—particularly in Table 3—shows that any definite trends are disguised by the fact that withdrawal responses are heavily concentrated in the working class stratum so that, generally, middle class adolescents, regardless of school type or political affiliations, record both more satisfied and dissatisfied replies. At the same time for the Labour party adolescents there is a close proximity between lower middle and skilled working class replies which prevents any divergence between the two broad class categories. This contrasts with the information for status aspirations when each of the three middle class strata had noticeably higher role aspirations than the two working class categories.

There is in fact a slight tendency for the working class Tories to be more hostile to the *status quo* than their middle class peers. The interesting differences, however, are between the secondary modern and grammar school pupils. The working class Conservatives at the grammar schools are strong advocates of the desirability of continuing the 11+ examination, which is in direct opposition to all the secondary modern pupils, regardless of their party label. It is quite rational to assess favourably those facets of the social system which have been instrumental in securing social mobility. Similar trends, although somewhat muted, occur with the question of the equitability of class relations. In summary, therefore, it is impossible to make accurate general statements about the likely responses of these particular crosspressured adolescents. The most one can hope for is to point out the rather special reactions of certain groups, reactions which appear to be guided by self-interest.

Another form of crosspressuring follows from the relationship between the parents' and the child's political party affiliations. Individuals who reject their parental labels are caught between the demands of their new identification and the family's traditional allegiances. The intensity of this will vary from family to family depending on the political awareness of the parents and the child. The concept of over-identification suggests the two following hypotheses.

H1 Adolescents with Labour party preferences, and parents whose
loyalties are both Conservative or Liberal, will record more
dissatisfied responses than adolescents from families in which all
party affiliations are Labour.

H2 Adolescents with Conservative party preferences, and parents
whose loyalties are both Labour or Liberal, will record more
satisfied responses than adolescents from families in which all
party affiliations are Conservative.

These two hypotheses assume that the adolescent faced with an unsympathetic family environment is likely to identify more positively
with his new-found loyalties than those from families in which no
such conflict exists; over-identification is a result of both the hostile
parents and the means by which the child counteracts their influence.

The central point about these hypotheses is that they make some
assessment on the changing relationship between party identifications
and attitudes. What happens to the attitudes of those adolescents
who have broken away from well established, family party preferences? Is there a difference between their attitudes and those of the
adolescents who maintain the family tradition? At the bottom of such
questions is an attempt to grapple with the implication of a political
party identification. There is a realization that individual attachments can be interpreted in differing ways; a party label does not
mean the same thing to all the faithful. A complex variety of
phenomena may be built into a party loyalty, including, for example,
status concerns, as well as the more usual ideological suppositions.
If this is the case certain labels may retain more hold than others;
their tentacles represent a wider range of commitments. The course
of change is by no means automatically in one direction: changes in
attitudes may precede, rather than follow, new political allegiances.

Both hypotheses 1 and 2 are invalidated by the evidence in Table 5.
If anything the reverse process takes place, for although political
party labels may have changed, little else has. The replies give the
following scale: if party affiliations are constant throughout the
family, then the adolescent is most likely to form attitudes which
have been associated with his particular party identification; if the
adolescent has a different party label from his parents his responses
to the attitudinal questions will still follow quite closely the trend
which has been connected with their party loyalties; and finally if he
has a positive party affiliation, in spite of apparent political apathy

TABLE 5

Attitudes and Rebellion from Parental Affiliations

M.	F.	A.[29]	Education			Jobs			Politics			Class			
			Sat.	Dis.	With.	Sat.	Dis.	With.	Sat.	Dis.	With.	Sat.	Dis.	With.	Total
			%	%	%	%	%	%	%	%	%	%	%	%	Ns.
L	L	L	19	58	23	35	37	28	42	27	31	17	50	22	363
C	C	C	27	62	11	38	39	23	40	39	21	37	38	25	230
C	C	L	33	50	17	33	44	23	61	22	17	35	39	28	18
L	L	C	22	68	10	36	45	19	32	45	23	16	55	19	31
NP	NP	L	30	49	21	30	33	37	33	33	34	30	31	39	64
NP	NP	C	22	53	25	29	46	25	39	34	27	32	43	25	41

[29] The symbols are translated as follows: M=mother, F=father, A=adolescent, L=Labour, C=Conservative, and NP=no party label. In the cases where there is rebellion from uniform parental preferences then L=uniform Labour or Liberal party labels, and C=uniform Conservative or Liberal preferences.

on the part of his parents, then he records a high percentage of withdrawal responses. For all four questions the Conservative party adolescents, with either Labour or Liberal parents, have fewer satisfied and more dissatisfied responses than where there is uniform commitment to the Conservative party. In three of the four questions the Labour party adolescents, with Conservative or Liberal parents, have fewer dissatisfied and more satisfied responses than where there is a uniform family allegiance to the Labour party.[30]

In the light of the American work on this subject it is not too surprising to see that the family influences attitudes as well as the formation of party labels. Easton and Hess argue that both political attitudes and values are formulated quite early: 'The truly formative years of the maturing member of a political system would seem to be the years between 3 and 13.'[31] Froman maintains that through this time period the attitudes of the child, '. . . increase in intensity, are more resistant to change and more likely to result in political behaviour.'[32] The previous chapter provided some evidence to support the claim that the potentially socially mobile adolescents may well reject the party loyalties of their parents. They have not also deserted, however, the ideological position associated with those parental loyalties.[33]

Another conflict situation arises when the political affiliations of the mother and father differ. Again the adolescent in such families is receiving contradictory messages and it is logical to suppose that he will resolve the dilemma by recording withdrawal responses. This assumes equal pulling power on the part of the parents and as there is no strong evidence in favour of this supposition the predicted conclusion is tentative.[34]

It is clear from Table 6 that withdrawal responses do not follow from conflicting family affiliations. For every single question

[30] The one exception is the question on job selection. Given the high percentage of Labour party adolescents at secondary modern schools and the likelihood of their leaving school at 15, this is not unexpected.

[31] D. Easton and R. Hess, 'The Child's Political World', *Midwest Journal of Political Science*, Volume 6, 1962, p. 236.

[32] Lewis A. Froman, 'Learning Political Attitudes', *Western Political Quarterly*, Volume 15, 1962, p. 312.

[33] This is assuming that reality matches this assumption. To substantiate this would require a study of the parents as well as their offspring.

[34] Women are generally less interested in politics but this study shows that the working class children are more inclined to take the party label of the mother than the father. On this see above, p. 98.

TABLE 6

Attitudes and Conflicting Family Affiliations

	Education		Jobs		Politics		Class		Total
	Pos.	With.	Pos.	With.	Pos.	With.	Pos.	With.	Ns.
	%	%	%	%	%	%	%	%	
Conflicting affiliations[35]	85	15	74	26	83	17	76	24	107
Constant Labour	77	23	72	28	69	31	67	33	363
Constant Conservative	89	11	77	23	79	21	75	25	230
Constant Liberal	90	10	71	29	83	17	79	21	42

[35] Only Labour, Conservative and Liberal party affiliations have been included.

the adolescents from such families are more willing to express opinions than those from families in which uniform Labour party
affiliations prevail. This is undoubtedly due to the relationship of
other influences to political preferences: the Labour party is linked
closely to the working class, secondary modern and comprehensive
school adolescents.

From all the attitudinal questions it is possible to make more
straightforward statements about the impact of the socialization
agents upon positive and withdrawal responses than the satisfied/dis-
satisfied pattern. There are strong overlaps along these lines. Coming
from a working class family, entering the secondary modern school,
and failing to establish a party loyalty tends to provide withdrawal
responses; while the middle class adolescent who attends grammar
school and has a definite party preference forms positive responses.
There is, therefore, the usual crystallizing of influences as well as the
modifying of impact through the interaction of the variables. A good
example of this latter point is the influence of the grammar school
upon the working class pupil. The big difficulty with the satisfied/
dissatisfied dimension is that so many of the hypotheses and assumptions are either invalidated or only weakly corroborated. There is
not the expected sharp break between the Labour and Conservative
party youths, working and middle class adolescents, and the grammar
and secondary modern pupils. Finally the evidence failed to validate
any of the statements about over-identification.

Although the notion of a smooth, coherent structuring of attitudes
appears to be unrealistic, there are still radically contrasting levels
of involvement in the society. The outsiders have been located and
there is some understanding of the mechanisms which create them.
According to a number of different measures, their future involvement is likely to be negligible. Furthermore even the participating
adolescents are inclined to be hostile, rather than favourably dis-
posed, towards the *status quo*. Neither trend suggests that we are
describing a civic culture or a stable democracy. Either these two
terms must be redefined to the point where they become almost meaningless, or it should be accepted that the society faces more critical
problems in terms of its basic support than has generally been recognized in the past.

9

THE HOME, SCHOOL AND
POLITICAL LOYALTIES

The main objective of this chapter is to illustrate the strength of the correlations between the socializing influences and the attitudinal questions. The technique is identical to that employed in Chapter Six.[1] There are the following subdivisions of the variables:

Independent and Control Variables[2]

1. Class: middle and working class adolescents
2. School: grammar and secondary modern school pupils in the tripartite system, and the three stream comparisons in Southern Comprehensive.
3. Political affiliations: comparisons between those with and without party labels for positive/withdrawal responses, and Labour and Conservative party contrasts for satisfied/dissatisfied responses.

Dependent Variables

1. The positive/withdrawal dimension.
2. The satisfied/dissatisfied dimension.

[1] For a full discussion of the technique employed and its limitations see above, pp. 88–90.

[2] All the relevant data, on which the calculations have been based, has been presented in the previous chapter. The nul hypothesis is still assumed: that there are no differences in the responses of middle and working class adolescents, grammar and secondary modern pupils, etc. Naturally the size of the sample varies: positive/withdrawal responses involves all the adolescents while the satisfied/dissatisfied responses concern just the two major

The Positive/Withdrawal Dimension

The 11+

Significant Differences

	The Tripartite Schools	Southern Comprehensive
Class	Not significant	Not significant
School	0·01	Not applicable
Stream	Not applicable	Not significant
Political affiliations	0·01	Not significant

Nearly all adolescents, regardless of their class background, are influenced by this examination. Therefore they all have some stake in expressing an opinion. The impact of school and political affiliations in the tripartite system is very specific: it centres upon the secondary modern, working class adolescents for political affiliations, and the middle class pupils with party loyalties for schools. Immediately there is confirmation of previous patterns; the meshing together of the socialization agents, and the fact that the secondary modern school more effectively depress middle class responses than the grammar schools elevate those of their working class pupils.[3]

The comprehensive school stands out by the complete lack of significant differences. Although there may not be distinctive response patterns, at least all the evidence is in the expected direction: most positive replies emanate from the middle class adolescents with party preferences who are top stream pupils, while withdrawal responses are closely tied to the juxtaposed groups. This is important, for a large number of subsamples are involved, and in view of the minute differences it is unusual that they should be so consistently in the same direction.

---

political parties. The Liberals may feel they are slighted but the two largest groups are observed; the small size of the Liberals sample makes it difficult to conduct the statistical test especially as the number of controls ensures that even this small number shrinks to smaller proportions. This also perpetuates previous goals as most of the hypotheses predicted the pattern of Conservative and Labour party responses.

[3] Working class, secondary modern school adolescents without party preferences have significantly more withdrawal responses than working class, secondary modern school adolescents with party preferences; this shows the congealing of socialization agents. Furthermore there are significant contrasts between the grammar and secondary modern school middle class pupils with established party loyalties; this confirms the sensitivity of middle class children to school placement.

Criteria Determing Job Placement and Promotion

Significant Differences

	The Tripartite Schools	Southern Comprehensive
Class	Not significant	Not significant
School	Not significant	Not applicable
Stream	Not applicable	0·01
Political affiliations	Not significant	Not significant

Although none of the differences in the tripartite system is significant, at least the trend is once more in the projected direction. It is hard for many of the working class youths at secondary modern schools to cast aspersions upon the work-a-day world that they are about to enter. Grievances are much more likely to be expressed on the basis of present experience. Gallup has gathered information which shows the cynicism of 18 to 20-year-old youths in relation to their work experiences; at the same time most were happy with the school they used to attend.[4]

In Southern Comprehensive even streaming has a restricted impact in spite of the overall significant differences; it differentiates sharply only two groups—the middle and working class youths who have party labels. Generally, however, withdrawal responses are high regardless of the comparisons which are made.

The Political System

Significant Differences

	The Tripartite Schools	Southern Comprehensive
Class	0·05	Not significant
School	0·01	Not applicable
Stream	Not applicable	0·02
Political affiliations	0·01	0·01

For the first time there are several significant differences as well as trends which are in the expected direction. In the selective secondary schools the impact of both class and political affiliations is

[4] Gallup directed their questions at a national sample of 1041 youths, aged 18 to 20. Over 70% were satisfied with their school and 88% at least fairly satisfied with the education they had received. This contrasts vividly with the 66% who *agreed* with this question, 'It has been said that what counts today is not what you do or how hard working you are but whom you know and how much influence you have.' See Social Surveys (Gallup Ltd.), *Report No. 89*, London, 1967, pp. 143–6.

specific, rather than general.[5] If the extent and consistency of the differences are taken into consideration then school type has pride of place. Similar comments are applicable to the comprehensive school. Besides class variations being small there are two noticeable reversals of expectations: in the top and third streams the middle class adolescents are less likely to express an opinion than the working class pupils.[6] This is an excellent example of the diminishing importance of class within the streams of the comprehensive school. This does not mean that family background has no influence in shaping the attitudes of the comprehensive schoolchildren but that their streams contain a relatively homogeneous group of individuals, undifferentiated by social class. This class range of responses within each stream may have differed when the child first entered the school but by now they have been phased out.[7] Although total political affiliation differences are significant, the important contrasts arise within the second stream.[8] For this question, therefore, streaming is the single most important factor in shaping the responses of the comprehensive school pupils.

Class Relations

Significant Differences

	The Tripartite Schools	Southern Comprehensive
Class	Not significant	Not significant
School	0·01	Not applicable
Stream	Not applicable	0·02
Political affiliations	Not significant	Not significant

The above values are a clear affirmation of all the previous comments: the class distinctions are small and in fact inconsistent; those resulting from political affiliations are consistent but none the less still

[5] Class distinctions occur only in the secondary modern schools but affect adolescents both with and without party loyalties. With political affiliations the differences are for the middle class, grammar and working class, secondary modern pupils. Once more the notion of interlocking influences has been vindicated for it is the working class, secondary modern youths without party preferences who have an especially large percentage of withdrawal responses.

[6] In the top stream this is true just of those adolescents with party labels; in the third stream it applies only to those without party loyalties.

[7] This indicates the need for socialization research which has a much longer time span.

[8] This applies to both working and middle class groups.

slight, while in striking contrast school and streaming reveal a persistent pattern associated with large differences. Although the questions on class and politics received an almost identical number of withdrawal responses there are good reasons for the particular concentration of withdrawal replies in relation to the class question. One would think that the adolescent is directly aware of the manifestations of class. At the same time class is a technical concept which may not be understood by all the 14-year-old schoolboys. It is not easy for the professional sociologist to interpret the various connotations it has. It is conceivable that many respondents, not understanding the term, refrained from replying. If this is so then school and streaming understandably should prove to be the main determinant of either positive or withdrawal responses. Those most favourably situated in the educational hierarchy have both the higher I.Q.s. as well as greater exposure to such concepts. In some ways this is a great pity for although the bottom stream, secondary modern pupils may not use the term 'class', they are probably fully aware of its actual implication. This is one area where the pilot study failed to serve its purpose; or alternatively its results were not interpreted with sufficient care.

It is legitimate to think of degrees of participation in the society, and there are certain groups for whom participation is so low that it is realistic to describe them as alienated from the mainstream of society. These are also the very adolescents destined for the most menial status roles. Their position stems from a variety of aspects within the socialization process; for certain adolescents there is a steady increase in their commitment, while for others there is an equally inevitable movement in the direction of their exclusion. The exclusion is a product of the increasing crystallization of the socialization agents; in the secondary moderns and bottom streams of the comprehensive schools the working class youths without party loyalties record more withdrawal responses than even closely related social groups.

As with aspirations, school and stream appear to be the most influential variables. There is less stress on the home environment as the major determinant of behaviour. The initial model constructed in Chapter Two suggested, and this is confirmed by the evidence, that it is unrealistic to think of socialization without some understanding of how the various agents interrelate with one another. However, within this complex process influences increase and decrease in their importance; by the age of 14 the school appears to have substantially modified, if not supplanted the impact of the home. The following chart, which summarizes the evidence, clearly suggests this point.

Positive—Withdrawal Responses[9]

	11+	Jobs	Politics	Class
The Tripartite Schools				
Class			×	
Political affiliations	×		×	
School	×		×	×
Southern Comprehensive				
Class				
Political affiliations			×	
Stream	×		×	×

The Satisfied/Dissatisfied Dimension

In view of the previous fluctuations it is not too disconcerting to discover that there is no consistency when it comes to assessing the relative importance of the socializing agents. There is no one combination which has a special association with either satisfied or dissatisfied replies. It makes more sense, therefore to consider the specialised items and the general direction of the data, rather than present the differences for each question.

In the comprehensive school, regardless of the independent variable, there are no statistically significant differences for any of the four questions and precious few definite trends. Regardless of the way the variables are correlated, the comprehensive school adolescents are a far more homogeneous group than their contemporaries in the tripartite system. This is partly a result of the fact that the comprehensive system is represented by only one school with a rather special location.[10] As the selective secondary schools are found in widely differentiated areas it is natural that their pupils should show a greater range of replies but the more vital distinction is the contrasting educational experiences the two types of schools promote.

Although there is plenty of research to illustrate how the 11+ has handicapped the working class child, he is no more likely to be dis-

[9] An × indicates there are statistically significant differences.
[10] On this see above. pp. 53–54.

satisfied with the examination than the middle class youth. This selection provokes general antagonism; the greater antipathy shifting constantly from middle to working class groups. The difference between the Labour and Conservative party adolescents is for the middle class grammar school, and the working class secondary modern, adolescents. In the grammar school it is the Labour party which is associated with antagonism to the 11+, while in the secondary moderns the Conservatives are in this position.[11] The working class Tory is not as subservient as is generally assumed. It is the crosspressured individuals, therefore, who show the greatest antipathy towards the 11+.

The continuation of selection for entry into the secondary schools, at least in its present form, is naturally far less appealing to the secondary modern than to the grammar school pupils. The largest differences are among the Conservatives, and this is true of both middle and working class schoolchildren. There is a clear division, therefore, between the haves and the have-nots. The Conservative party could alienate a large number of its supporters, both present and future, by its somewhat nebulous stand on the issue of selective education. Of course it does not seem to prevent a commitment in the present circumstances, which raises the whole issue of the rationality of party allegiances. In addition it is conceivable that those who are hostile to the 11+ may still favour some form of selection, or oppose selection but disapprove of the present alternative.

The analysis reaffirms that those with Labour party loyalties are more inclined than the Conservatives to accept that the government is responsible to the people. The relevant chi square values may not be significant but they show a distinct trend; as this occurs so rarely it is an important point.[12] Although there is this trend, it unfortunately contradicts initial assumptions which linked pro status responses to the Conservative party.

With the class question the variables come closest to fulfilling the necessary requirement of persistently significant differences, but the most intense dissatisfied responses come from the crosspressured

[11] Of course those individuals with Labour party labels are also hostile to the 11+ so it comes as something of a surprise that there should be statistically significant differences between the Conservatives and themselves.

[12] This applies to both the tripartite and comprehensive schools. The one exception is the middle class, top stream pupils; in this case the Conservatives have more sympathy with the political system.

individuals, which suggests it is more in tune with the spirit of the data to think of specific impacts.[13]

The questions are interpreted in what can only be described as a highly realistic manner: there is the antagonism of the secondary modern adolescents towards the 11+ examination, working class hostility to the structure of class relations, and the strong feeling on the part of the Labour party youths that the government is responsible to the people.[14] Besides this point, assessing the relative impact of the variables does not result in many consistent patterns. Scarce resources are also a reality for those who are in the process of receiving system rewards and they record more dissatisfaction, as well as more satisfaction, with the *status quo* than those who receive the most meagre returns from the society. Of course withdrawal responses do not automatically imply apathy; for these individuals there may well be more pertinent ways of reaping vengeance than filling in the appropriate boxes of a questionnaire!

Overriding all the other evidence is that which points out the extreme isolation of certain groups of individuals in conjunction with the widespread dislike of society's present structure. Low future role aspirations, negligible potential participation and current social disabilities present a formidable and depressing picture of an important segment of this society. The position of the crosspressured stratum varies from aspirations to the attitudinal questions; with aspirations they bridge the gap between the large harmoniously socialized groups; for attitudes they adopt a quite distinctive, usually anti-system, stance.

[13] The real contrasts are between the crosspressured and harmoniously socialized adolescents: the middle class, grammar school Conservatives and the middle class, grammar school Labour party identifiers; middle class, grammar school Conservatives and middle class, secondary modern school Tories.

[14] Realistic in the sense that they conform to my own, and hopefully others', assessment of their self-interest.

10

SOCIAL CHANGE AND THE STRATEGY OF EDUCATIONAL RESEARCH AND REFORM

The assumptions underlying the socialization model, constructed in Chapter Two, are straightforward: within every society there are mechanisms to ensure its stability and perpetuation. Many of the experiences which apparently aim at the individual's development also have the wider objective of maintaining social harmony. In most societies the central socializing agent is the family but in the industrialized nations its functions have been increasingly shared with other institutions, especially with the educational system. The position of the educational system owes much to the growth of industry. There is a need for large segments of the population to acquire skills which can no longer be learnt within the family. As the requirements of industry grow more sophisticated, the link between the type of things learned in the family and the demands of industry grow ever more fragile. In the late nineteenth century there was a growing threat to Britain's industrial supremacy from the Germans and the Americans. The 1870 Education Act was viewed partially as a way to contain this threat; economic expansion required more skilled workers and a growing army of clerical staff. In the same way comprehensive education is sometimes seen as the twentieth century solution to our manpower problems; no longer will we fail to make use of all our talent.

Although there is not a direct link today between family training and job requirements, it is still true that individual job opportunities are closely bound by family background. Why has this taken place? Traditionally in England the school system has reaffirmed both social and academic differences between children. Of course these distinctions are very closely related to the child's family environment. It is these close connections which are responsible for different socialization experiences. The pattern of role aspirations generally confirms these assumptions: the middle class children who dominate the grammar schools are inclined to think of pursuing some form of further education, and aim for white collar jobs. This is all very different from the many working class children at the secondary moderns who focus upon skilled working class jobs or, at the very best, minor clerical or technical posts. The well-known stress at school upon the need to obtain paper qualifications adds to the firmness of these relations. As early as the junior schools, the sorting out process begins, for it is the top stream children who are coached to pass the 11+. In secondary schools G.C.E. passes are the prized possession; those with reasonable 'O' level performances will proceed to the sixth form and 'A' levels. The university represents the final stage in this selection process, and even at university there is the degree pecking order. Who are the failures: the secondary modern pupils, those who leave grammar school with few or no G.C.E. passes, those who have 'A' levels but fail to find a university place, or university students who end up with only a second class honours degree? The selection techniques are so numerous and refined that an absurdly complex success hierarchy could be established.

It is not only further education that is so dependent on past academic achievements. Increasingly the minimum criterion to be considered for many jobs is the possession of nationally recognized certificates. If anything, the pressures in this direction have intensified throughout the secondary schools with the introduction of the Certificate of Secondary Education (C.S.E.), a watered down G.C.E. which is now widely taken by secondary modern pupils. Although the evidence has not been set out in the past chapters, there is a strong tendency for the secondary modern pupils, who were thinking of taking up apprenticeships also to want to pass C.S.E. examinations. Is there now a norm that entry into apprenticeships is dependent upon prior examination success? The norm perhaps created informally by the school, the prospective employer, and the adolescents themselves? Given all the testing and chanelling that has taken place it is not at all surprising to find that the fourteen- and fifteen-year-old school children are realistic both about their prospects of further education and about job opportunities. In fact it is remarkable that so many lower stream, secondary modern pupils remain optimistic about their job chances. This may be one reason why Gallup poll found the majority of eighteen- to twenty-year-old youths highly cynical about the nature of job promotion: they start out with such high hopes that their chances of fulfilling them are slim. Failure directs attention towards the system's shortcomings rather than personal limitations.[1]

Political aspirations are interesting precisely because they do not follow this trend. Class, school and stream do not shape political aspirations in the same way as they determine educational and occupational goals. Perhaps middle class skills, to paraphrase Blondel, are a necessary part of the equipment of the contemporary politician, but it is still more of an 'amateur's profession' than many others of about the same status. We can more than tolerate the politician who has no university degree. Besides the important financial backing which trade unions will provide for many prospective M.P.s. there is also sanction from democratic norms for the working class, Labour party parliamentary candidate. Participation is a part of democratic theory and presumably it means participation by all segments of society rather than by the favoured middle class minority, even if it should be a rather large minority. Nearly all the youths in the study also adhered to one of the three major party labels. Apathy was very much the exception.[2] The same syndrome of social forces which is associated with low role aspirations also affects political apathy. Nevertheless there is effective political socialization, as defined by this limited criteria.

Apathy increases once the adolescent is asked to evaluate specific aspects of society. Just as the lack of a major party label may mean a number of different things, so various interpretations can be made about this unwillingness to evaluate major social institutions. It could be alienation, apathy, or simply confusion. Regardless of interpretations, it implies a lack of involvement with social issues. It is therefore much more important than the actual direction of positive responses. Satisfaction or dissatisfaction with the *status quo* indicates engagement with it. Isolation from involvement is far more difficult to break down.

---

[1] For the relevant Gallup information see above, p. 133.

[2] It may, of course, be something other than apathy—a dislike of all party ties, or, more precisely, of the accepted political parties. It is probably more accurate to reserve apathy only for those without party labels, but there are very few individuals who selected anything other than one of the three main parties.

Class, school, political interest and sex are all influences which shape the formation of aspirations and attitudes along very definite lines. The notion of working class deference is still widely accepted; for example, it is still one of the major explanations for the working class Tory. Certain of the secondary modern school headmasters who co-operated in this research, felt that the questionnaire would either not interest, or not be understood by, their lower stream pupils. Furthermore women, for all their twentieth-century emancipation, still have a restricted range of job opportunities. These same influences, however, do not point to any particular direction of commitment once the individual is prepared to evaluate social institutions. In the first place, scarce resources affect most individuals. Even an apparently favoured group, like the middle class, grammar school Tories, still have to accept, at times, a Labour Government. Why should they feel the government is responsible to the people when it may be in the process of implementing a set of policies to which they are completely opposed? It is difficult to imagine anyone forming an affective relationship to society without also receiving accompanying instrumental benefits. What is important is that no one sizeable group should continually receive only the most meagre rewards. What the socialization model implies, and the evidence confirms, is that this is the unenviable position of a particular stratum within this society.

The contrasting responses to the questions on status aspirations and attitudes towards social institutions suggest that it makes sense to view socialization in a variety of different ways, each dependent on the type of issue under observation. The status crystallization thesis is supported by the data on role aspirations. There is an interlocking of influences to ensure a smooth flow from the past to the present and into the future; at each stage in this socialization model there is a confirmation of earlier experiences. However, when we turn to the evaluation of social institutions, Richard Rose's findings on Manchester University undergraduates, as well as more recent student revolts, suggest that parental attitudes are being discarded. Although there is no positive proof, the evidence of this study suggests that a similar rejection of parents is taking place at earlier stages in the life cycle. It is the crosspressured adolescents who are most inclined to disown the *status quo*, especially if it is structured in such a way to work against their own interests. Crosspressuring implies stresses and strains for these adolescents; they have a heightened awareness because of their position in the social hierarchy. For university students, dissatisfaction probably stems from a combination of events: besides the university cutting loose the undergraduate from his family and local ties, it exposes him to a new form of education, one which ideally encourages a dispassionate appraisal of the world around him.[3] In some respects there is a close affinity between our adolescents and undergraduates—neither have yet entered the work-a-day world. In fact the fourteen-year-old secondary modern boy may be much closer to this experience than the first year university student. Due to prolonged education some youths may be in their early twenties before they become adults in the full sense. They may be directed towards specific career goals but this is not true of everyone: for example, many students in the social sciences still have little idea of their eventual job. There is a continuous postponement of forming a job identity which, in Erik Erikson's terms, is the most important commitment any individual can make.[4] There do not appear to be many active radicals over the age of thirty. The stress now is upon the importance of particular phases in the socialization process. Earlier experiences may be challenged, and eventually undermined, by later events. There is a continuous fight for the individual's loyalties. Clearly this view can only be substantiated by research which has a considerable time span built into it and this makes the status confirmation model more appropriate for this study.

Even where there are good chances of a clash between the school and the home environment, there may not in reality be much of a conflict. Working class, grammar school pupils form three fairly distinctive groups. First there are those who readily adjust to the school and complete their secondary education with at least a certain amount of success.[5] The Jackson and Marsden study suggests that most of these youths come from families which already incorporate many of the essential grammar school values. There is likely to be an improvement in social status, a better job, and all the benefits which accompany this, but most of the children's values will remain similar to those of their parents. In fact both the family and the

[3] The list of potential radicalizing forces can be extended *ad infinitum*. Kenneth Kenniston presents an interesting social-psychological explanation. See Kenneth Kenniston, *The Young Radicals*, New York, Harcourt, 1968.

[4] On this see above, p. 46.

[5] For a fuller discussion of this point see above, pp. 31–32.

school are inculcating the same middle class success mores. In the second group there are those who are equally adept at accommodating to the school but achieve somewhat less academic success. They make use of their grammar school career but are unlikely to want to go to university. They will be thinking about the following kinds of employment: apprenticeships, clerical and minor technical jobs, and in some cases an executive post.[6] At the other end of the continuum are the problem boys. They are unsympathetic to grammar school values and have little interest in educational attainment. Although there is a clash between the school and home environments of these adolescents, it is less certain how many of them actually experience this and for how long it remains an important influence in their lives. There is a gradual evolution of defence mechanisms which form a strong protection against the enemy, i.e. the school. The most important defence is the peer group culture, which not only provides potential protection against school authority but also becomes the youth's reference point. His behaviour is then aimed at pleasing his peers rather than the school. In many ways the schools themselves encourage this development: there is an acceptance that these pupils are not going to be among the high achievers; they are put in the bottom streams where few, if any, pressures are applied to them; and it is widely felt, perhaps even hoped, that they will leave school as soon as is legally permitted. The tentative suggestion, therefore, is that after the initial confrontation between the home and the school there follows a far longer period in which both sides gradually disengage from the battle.[7] The end result is mutual indifference. If there is little interaction between the home and the school, then the impact of early family socialization will remain dominant. Nothing has arisen to shake its hold. Rather than challenge those early influences, the school actually modifies its structure to allow them to flourish. With more probing, therefore, this last category of working class grammar schoolchildren, may in fact represent a perfect illustration of the status crystallisation concept of socialization, the first of the two models posed in this chapter.

Socialization is not simply a process by which individuals come to learn, accept and act upon socially approved values. It is also a study of how various institutions within the society perpetuate and trans-

[6] The executive class of the civil service is a good example of this type of job.
[7] This evolution is suggested in the work of Colin Lacey, see above, pp. 16–17.

mit these values. With all social survey research there is a danger that in the eagerness to describe the response patterns, explanations of why they should be like this tend to be ignored. If support for the political institutions is high, then the next logical question is to see why this should be so. Unless there is some conception of how behaviour is structured by society, then drawing conclusions about the nature of that society from survey data is rather meaningless. To begin with the supposition that a democracy is under observation and then proceed more or less directly to the analysis of the questionnaires, concluding that this illustrates the requirements for stable democracy, leaves out the crucial step of explaining what this particular way of organising society is supposed to achieve.[8] Furthermore it is proving the obvious, for if this is indeed the democratic society then these cannot help but be the democratic citizens in the making. Democracy will be seen in one's findings, no matter what they are.

It is fair to conclude, on the basis of this study, that the stability of English society is dependent upon the way the educational system channels people into contrasting roles. It means that quite large minorities have relatively bleak futures: the rudiments of an education, low status and poorly paid jobs, and little participation in political affairs. It must be remembered that these people pay the price for the benefits which the rest of us enjoy. Change *and* stability, participation *and* non-participation, high *and* low role aspirations are complementary parts of one process; in fact they help to define each other.

In England there does not appear to be an acceptance of the principle that there are desirable rewards which should encompass all citizens. There is an attempt to legitimate a social hierarchy in which some of us are very much more equal than others! The study suggests that the legitimating devices require attention, for even on the part of those whom the society rewards there is still a considerable amount of dissatisfaction. There is some recognition that the hierarchy is not on a firm footing, that placement within it is partially dependent upon inequitable selection procedures in the educational system, at work and in the class structure.

[8] For a more detailed discussion of this, see above pp. 122–124.

SOCIAL CHANGE

Educational Reform and Social Change

Invariably both politicians and sociologists view educational reform as an attempt to ameliorate the socialization experiences of individuals: to improve job and educational opportunities, to make the child more aware of the society around him and thus increase his sense of involvement and commitment. As the first chapter showed, these ideals have been associated with the movement towards comprehensive education. Now there is a growing recognition that perhaps it is not going to usher in the millenium after all. The only disconcerting aspect of the whole debate is that there should have been such naïve hopes in the first place. After all it is not so long ago that people were claiming that the 1944 Education Act had introduced 'secondary education for all' and established 'parity of esteem' between the various forms of secondary education. In spite of these shortcomings most interested persons still consider the act to be a big move in the right direction, instrumental in creating an educational system which extended to more schoolchildren than ever before the chance of decent schooling. Furthermore there was a genuine attempt to ensure equality of educational opportunity; the 11+ is not an ideal selection device but surely it is better that this should govern entry into the grammar schools rather than the right to pay, which had dominated the pre-Second World War educational structure?[9] Is it not possible that comprehensive education, although not fulfilling the dreams of its more enthusiastic proponents, will nevertheless result in a number of not inconsequential changes?

What are the innovations which the comprehensive schools, or rather, those in this particular study, are introducing? In the first place the social class of the pupils appears to be less of a constraint in the formation of role aspirations. Within any one stream the middle and working class adolescents compete on more or less equal terms. In the grammar schools this did not happen: even in the top streams, which after all are a very select stratum of the total I.Q. scale, the middle class children have noticeably higher role aspirations than their working class peers. The comprehensive schools, therefore, may well encourage the growth of a true meritocracy. An additional change is the general widening of opportunities; the second stream

[9] Of course there was a grammar scholarship system before 1945 but nowhere near as extensive as that evolving from the 1944 Education Act.

pupils, for example, have much higher aspirations than the adolescents at secondary modern schools.[10] The large second stream at Southern Comprehensive performs two functions: it stimulates the aspirations of its working class pupils and provides a cushion for the less intelligent middle class youths. These are undoubtedly very important educational developments for they extend the range of opportunities. It is probable that many of these children would not have fared so well in a selective scheme.

Of course a price has to be paid for these developments, and it is the fact that the traditional outcasts appear to bear the costs of the system, which forms the core of this critique of comprehensive education. Selective secondary education tends to confirm class differences, while in the comprehensive schools it is the streaming hierarchy which accomplishes this task. The individuals in the bottom streams are a very carefully defined group. They are at the end of a much longer scale than is the case in either the grammar or secondary modern schools. These individuals who have little chance of making it within the system are grouped together to form a little world of their own, a school within the school. The central problem—what to do with the potential non-achievers—is not tackled in an especially original way. Separating, even more carefully, the sheep from the goats involves little more than carrying present values to their logical conclusion. The comprehensive schools are still taking the easy path of harmonizing with, rather than challenging, the family.

The next logical question to raise is, 'What is to be done?' Of course there is no one simple answer. At first sight it seems reasonable to advocate the cause of further structural reform: that the changeover to comprehensive education should be paralleled by the abolition of academic streaming. This issue has generated an enormous amount of controversy. *The Times* feels it is one of the two major controversies in education; 'it is called "streaming" and will be fought out between those who think it necessary to group pupils by ability in comprehensive schools, if the academic standards at the grammar schools and independent schools are to be maintained in a comprehensive system, and those who believe that the full academic and social benefits of comprehensive reorganization are not to be had so

[10] These are roughly comparable categories. The second stream at Southern Comprehensive is very large and undoubtedly contains a small minority of adolescents who would have gone to grammar schools.

long as streaming is practised.'[11] In conclusion this editorial claims: 'No one should be encouraged to believe that a mere change to non-streaming would bring realization of the hopes which a mere change to non-selective secondary schools is fast disappointing. In this, as in everything else, the skill and sympathy of the teacher, and the ethics of his school, matters far more to his pupils than the type of organization that administrators, politicians, or social engineers wish on him.'[12] It is clear that structural reform cannot achieve all the objectives which have been held out for comprehensive education. Although there has been a failure to spell out all the difficulties—on the part of both politicians and social engineers—it is doubtful if even the most ardent supporters of comprehensive education would in fact credit 'a mere change to non-selective secondary schools' as providing the total solution.

The stress on the role of the teacher reflects the findings of an expensive study conducted by the National Foundation for Educational Research.[13] It must have always been obvious that teachers' attitudes were crucial to the success or failure of any form of school organisation. A more important criticism is the implicit acceptance of the concept of 'ability' almost as if it were separate from the techniques which are devised to ascertain it. Intelligence testing was rejected in these words: 'There were two main reasons for not allocating children to groups on the basis of intelligence. Firstly, there was no group test available which was sufficiently reliable for use with children aged seven-plus. Secondly, it is doubtful whether tests of intelligence measure something different from attainment tests.'[14] Finally Lunn settled for the following measure of ability: 'Since the Reading test was the one most free from curriculum-bias, "ability" was defined in terms of initial reading score corrected for age, and pupils were allocated to one of the three ability groups on this basis.'[15] Intelligence tests are also subjected to the following criticism: 'The work of Hebb (1949), Piaget (1952) and Bloom

[11] *The Times*, 28th January, 1970. *The Times* comments in rather simplistic terms, for example, 'a mere change to non-streaming' and 'a mere change to non-selective secondary schools'. They must be unaware of the enormous political and educational controversy which has surrounded these 'mere innovations'! Or perhaps emotion is clouding judgment. The other major area of disagreement, *The Times* feels, concerns the relative status of the various institutions of higher education. [12] *ibid.*

[13] Joan C. Barker Lunn, *Streaming in the Primary School*, N.F.E.R., Slough, Bucks, 1970. [14] *ibid.*, p. 58. [15] *ibid.*, p. 58.

(1964) has shown that intelligence is not fixed but grows and develops and this is partly dependent on environmental stimulation. It can be regarded as a fluid collection of skills which are to a considerable extent developed by early experience, and subsequently affected by the quality and length of formal schooling that an individual undergoes.'[16] Surely much the same objections can be directed at any attempt to ascertain 'ability' by a reading test. Lunn would probably accept that she is measuring a changing characteristic which is dependent on environmental stimulus as well as innate ability. Later Lunn presents the results of a battery of tests designed to ferret out divergent thinking. Not unexpectedly the 'highly creative' group correlates highly with children of average and above average 'ability'.[17] The important point is that there is no perfect correlation; average ability (as opposed to above-average ability) and high creativity are quite common links. Surely the point is that there are almost as many different forms of ability as there are people. What in fact has generally passed as ability, even in Lunn's study, is simply a measure of what is required to do well in our schools. Once such concepts are employed, the hierarchical system is just up the stairs. There is only a limited amount of ability, measured in such and such a way, available; to ensure its preservation the talented few must be separated. The fact that Lunn finds approximately one child in six has been placed in the 'wrong' stream even at the end of the school year is not necessarily an argument in favour of non-streaming; it could be assumed that what are required are more carefully devised tests to ensure that mistakes of this type do not occur.

In the hands of the expert, the findings of the educational psychologists can be usefully employed. Unfortunately they provide ammunition to all and sundry, which results in partial interpretations and misleading impressions. Reporting on Lunn's work *The Times* had this to say: 'One child in six in streamed primary schools is in the wrong stream at the end of the school year, according to a report published yesterday by the National Foundation for Educational Research. They are either better than many children in the stream above them or worse than many in the stream below.'[18] It is not until

---

[16] *ibid.*, p. 58. Vernon, however, actually suggests that, in spite of all their limitations, intelligence tests are subjected to less class bias than most of the ways in which children have been separated.   [17] *ibid.*, p. 80.
[18] Article by the education correspondent of *The Times*, 28th January, 1970.

the following paragraph that we find out in terms of what criteria they are better or worse: 'At the start of the next year only about a quarter of the wrongly-placed pupils are moved into their correct stream: the rest, on the basis of their performance in English and Arithmetic, remain in the wrong stream.'[19] There is, therefore, only indirect reference to the ability measure, and as in Lunn's book, the subsequent passages consequently mention children of average or below average ability.

It is true that social change does not stem from structural manipulation of the educational system alone. Yet it is hard to see how social change can be introduced without fulfilling this minimum requirement. All the progressive ideals in the world are fruitless unless they are accompanied by the reform of social institutions. Ideals have to have a favourable context in which they can be implemented. It is true that teachers who are unsympathetic to streaming may do more harm than good in non-streamed schools but there is the question of how teachers' attitudes can be changed. It is possible that those who believe in selection may have their outlook reaffirmed by teaching experiences in non-streamed schools, but is it not also possible that the new environment may stimulate them to think again? Furthermore how many teachers have to be convinced of the merits of non-selection before streaming arrangements can be modified? Must all first be converted, and change proceed at the pace of the most unprogressive element within the profession?

If educational reform has certain social goals, it must none the less not lose sight of the question of academic attainment. Often different assessments are reached simply because the standards of evaluation are in conflict. The schools are structured to ascertain individual levels of academic attainment; the frequent internal (end of term) and external (usually university controlled) examinations make this very clear to the child, parents, teachers and other interested parties such as employers. This objective dominates the schools because of the close relationship between educational attainment and job opportunities. In her pessimistic conclusion on the consequences of comprehensive education, Julienne Ford states: 'This raises (again) the question of the functions of the educational system and its relationship with the whole society. For clearly the schools serve not only to provide children with a relatively uniform socialization—to teach them aspects of a *common* culture—but also to provide them

[19] *ibid.*

with *differential* socialization. It is through the educational system that selection and differential training for major adult roles are effected. And while the burden of distribution of personnel in the occupational structure lies in the schools they will be unable to avoid selection and segregation.'[20] Can the two sets of goals–the desire for more social equality and the improvement of academic standards–be reconciled?

In order to alter the *status quo* it is helpful to have some knowledge of its origins. There are few who would deny that intelligence is an important determinant of academic performance, even if the only measure of that intelligence is an I.Q. test.[21] If intelligence is primarily a function of inheritance then what differences, if any, can educational change make to the extension of academic attainment? Surely it can at least provide a system which will allow every child to realize his inherited ability, for as Sir Cyril Burt, that arch defender of the impact of hereditary variables, states, 'What deserves explicit mention is that within each class the range of individual differences is almost as wide as in the general population. Hence, since the manual class is much larger than the non-manual, there are far more gifted children in that class than in the middle or professional classes; and a large proportion of them still fail to secure the education they deserve.'[22] What this study shows is that the comprehensive schools could well be implementing this programme: extending opportunities to all those with the required 'ability', while making it quite clear to those who are unfortunately not so gifted exactly where they stand.[23]

There are few who are so bold as to place a precise figure on how much intelligence owes to hereditary influences.[24] A more common view is to point out how inherited characteristics and the environment

[20] Julienne Ford, *Social Class and the Comprehensive School*, London, Routledge and Kegan Paul, 1969, p. 134.

[21] The whole question of the origins of intelligence has been reopened with the publication of the Black Papers. See 'Black Paper No. One: The Fight for Education', and 'Black Paper No. Two: The Crisis in Education'. Both tracts were edited by C. B. Cox and A. E. Dyson and published as special issues of the *Critical Quarterly Society*, London, 1969.

[22] A letter to *The Sunday Times*, 8th February, 1970.

[23] This refers to the patterns within Southern Comprehensive.

[24] Jensen, in his well-publicized article on the respective 'abilities' of blacks and whites, is one of the few willing to do this. See Arthur R. Jensen, 'How Much Can We Boost I.Q. and Scholastic Achievement?', *Harvard Educational Review*, Volume 39, 1969, pp. 1–123.

interact with each other, and leave it at that.[25] It is fascinating to see that even the Secretary of State for Education and Science now has to be *au fait* with genetic theory. In the debate on the second reading of the Education Bill to compel all the local authorities to introduce comprehensive schemes, he had this to say: 'The intelligent quotient of a child is a function partly of inheritance and partly of environment and background. Environmental factors which most strongly influence a child's I.Q. are the qualities and amenities of the home, interest of the parents, the quality of the neighbourhood, the quality of the primary school, the size of the family, parental aspirations and so on. Thus I.Q. is an indication of the innate equipment, but it is also a measure of the social background and the two cannot be separated.'[26] Surely whatever theory of the origins of intelligence one subscribes to, there is precious little evidence that a comprehensive school, or even a non-streamed comprehensive school, will result in diminishing levels of educational attainment. The evidence of this study suggests quite the contrary—that comprehensive schools may well actually spread educational opportunities, thus raising the level of educational attainment. What is interesting is that this should be done within the framework of a highly selective milieu.

The decision that has to be reached is whether further advances can be made by abolishing streaming. Julienne Ford commenced with five propositions of which the third was: 'Under a comprehensive system of secondary education early selection does not occur to such a great extent.'[27] It is because this proposition is subverted that she concludes the comprehensive schools will not be capable of meeting their educational or social goals. She states, 'I would like to suggest that this is not necessarily the case. For it is possible to conceive of a school system which is freed of the distortions imposed by the selective function. Surely if we are to dream about Utopias (something which the proponents of "comprehensive" reform have certainly been doing) then we must be more imaginative. There is no point in tinkering with the type of selection which occurs in the schools, no point in replacing tripartite schools by schools which are no more than "multilateral". If we are to produce any change at all

[25] On this see above, pp. 14–16.

[26] As quoted in the *The Times*, 13th February, 1970.

[27] *op. cit.*, p. 11. Actually listed as the fifth proposition, but the second and third are really subsections of the first proposition.

we must completely free the schools of their function as selection agencies for occupation.'[28] Such a programme passes the boundaries of reality; education has nearly always been, and always will be, training for later life, which for most of us includes the necessity of working for a living. One powerful reason for the expansion in the educational system has been the spread of increasingly sophisticated techniques in the industrial process. The problem is that we have a differentiated job structure with a hierarchy of overlapping status and economic rewards.

In the past the educational system appears to have responded passively, caught between the demands of the economy and bowing down to the privileged few. There has been an increasing realization that success at school is very much dependent upon family background. Even the 11 + was an attempt to minimize these differences and the movement towards comprehensive education is another thrust in this direction. It would be a great pity if these gains were nullified by continuing with an outmoded goal—placing the child in a rigid hierarchy from the very day he first attends school. There is an increasing demand for more skilled manpower and multi-, rather than uni-dimensional talents. What selection does is to relate children at an early age to particular segments of the occupational hierarchy. It thereby severely limits the opportunities of those who happen to be placed at the bottom of the pile. If attention is concentrated upon certain occupational categories—those with the highest prestige—then it is possible to describe all the secondary modern pupils as 'failures', for their chances of reaching such elevated heights are very slim indeed. In these terms, therefore, the opportunities of approximatly 80 per cent of the children in maintained secondary schools have been severely limited by the selection process.

With the active co-operation of interested parties, above all the teachers, there should be a general movement towards non-selection in education.[29] There has been a shift in the right direction. Moreover this study and others show the impact of schooling structures.[30] There is little evidence that the most able of our schoolchildren

[28] op. cit., pp. 135–6.

[29] At least some teachers have been persuaded by the arguments in favour of non-selection. See, 'The Dossier on Streaming', *Teacher*, Volume 15, January 30th, 1970, pp. 12–13.

[30] Especially those studies that show how streaming becomes a self-fulfilling prophecy.

will suffer by this movement. Even Lunn's study did not show less 'ability' in the non-streamed schools.[31] However, there is plenty of evidence that suggests this would benefit many of those who have previously been denied both educational and job opportunities. The end result is favourable to these individuals and the society at large. It may be argued that even with its rigid streaming hierarchy, Southern Comprehensive is managing to do this. It must be possible, however, to extend some hope to the third stream adolescents. Or is the reservoir of talent, ability, intelligence–whatever you call it, or more important however you measure it–something which some people possess but others do not have?

The end result is not an egalitarian society. The educational system *per se* cannot possibly achieve this goal. As long as there is a hierarchy of rewards in the job market then there will be differentiation in the schools. Education must ensure that everyone has the opportunity to make the best use of his potential, and selection is a major barrier that must be removed. Of course what happens to those who are still thwarted in spite of a schooling system which allows everyone to fulfil his potential is another question. We are not all equal, and no matter how you manipulate the social system we never will be. By the time these aims are achieved perhaps we will have a different type of society, one in which although all men may not be equal, at least all their varying contributions will be equally regarded and equally rewarded.

[31] Lunn's study actually shows few 'ability' differentials regardless of school structure. I was thinking of a wider range of benefits than her restricted definition of 'ability'. In fact it is very difficult to assess accurately the impact of non-streaming. Firstly it is not easy to match either samples of adolescents or the schools. In addition transferring pupils from streamed to non-streamed schools is not the type of exercise to encourage as an experiment. Even if it were possible it would be hard to measure the impact of the change-over *per se*. Does behaviour alter simply because there is an experiment taking place?

APPENDIX

THE QUESTIONNAIRE
A STUDY OF ENGLISH SECONDARY SCHOOLS

The following questions are part of a study being made at the University of Manchester. The study is an attempt to learn about the opinions of pupils in secondary schools. This is *not* a test, so there are no right or wrong answers, therefore we are anxious that you answer the questions as carefully and truthfully as you can. Do *not* copy answers from your neighbour because we want *your* views and not his or hers. Most of the answers do not require a great deal of writing and in most questions you can indicate your choice by putting a little tick like this √. Remember tick *only one choice*, either that choice that best represents your own feelings or most truthfully describes your situation. Where the question requires some other answer than a simple tick it is quite clear what you have to do.

As you will see we do not ask for your name and so all your answers to the questions are absolutely private.

1. When were you born?

2. Where did you first live? Town
   County

3. Where do you live now? Town
   County

4. Have you lived in the same house all your life?
   Yes
   No

5. How many brothers or sisters do you have?

6. How many of your brothers or sisters have gone, or are still going, to grammar schools?

7. How many of your brothers or sisters have gone, or are still going, to secondary modern schools?

8. Have any of your brothers or sisters attended, or are still attending, other types of schools (that is other than secondary modern or grammar schools)? If they have could you tell me the type or types of schools they attend or used to attend?

9. Would you say that most of your friends go to the same school as yourself or attend other schools?
   1. Most of my friends go to my present school
   2. About half of my friends go to my present school
   3. Most of my friends are at other schools

10. What is your present form in this school?

11. *Would you like* to pass any examinations before leaving this school?
    1. Yes
    2. No

12. If you would like to pass some exams could you tell me what exams. Please list the subjects.
    'A' level G.C.E.'s
    'O' level G.C.E.'s
    Any other types of exams?

13. Of course, we do not always succeed in doing the things we should like to do. Do you *in fact expect* to pass any exams before leaving this school?
    1. Yes
    2. No

14. If you in fact expect to pass some exams could you tell me what exams. Please list the subjects.
    'A' level G.C.E.'s
    'O' level G.C.E.'s
    Any other types of exams?

15. When you have finished at your present school *would you like* to continue your education elsewhere?
    1. Yes
    2. No

16. If 'yes' could you tell me *at what kind of place* you would like to continue your education?

17. Do you *in fact expect* to continue your education when you have finished at your present school?
    1. Yes
    2. No

18. If 'yes' could you tell me *at what kind of place* you expect to continue your education?

19. What king of things are likely to prevent you from continuing your education at the place you would most like to go to?

20. At what age do you expect to be leaving school?

15	18
16	19
17	20 or over

21. Which of the following statements *best describes* the way you will feel when you leave school?
    1. Very glad to leave
    2. Glad to leave
    3. I will have mixed feelings
    4. Sorry to leave
    5. Very sorry to leave

22. Could you give the reasons why you have chosen this answer?

23. How interested would you say *you are* in your education?
    1. Very interested
    2. Interested
    3. Not very interested
    4. Bored

24. Do your parents ever discuss your school work with you?
    1. Frequently
    2. Occasionally
    3. Very rarely
    4. Never

25. As you know, most of the people at school have taken, or will take, an examination known as the 11+. What is your opinion of this examination?
    1. The 11+ examination should be abolished.
    2. Some changes should be made to the 11+ exam.
    3. I have no opinion one way or the other.
    4. The 11+ examination works fairly well.
    5. It is essential to have the 11+ examination.
    6. Don't know what to think.

26. Could you give the reasons why you have chosen this answer?

27. What do you think of the education you are receiving?
    1. It is the best education I could receive anywhere.
    2. On the whole I am satisfied with it.
    3. I have mixed feelings about it.
    4. I have been somewhat disappointed with it.
    5. I could have received a much better education elsewhere.

Now here is a somewhat different set of questions.

28. Speaking generally, what are the things about this country you are most proud of?

29. Aside from the people you know personally–of all the people you hear or read about–could you name one or more individuals you admire very much?

30. Often we look up to a person because of the type of job he has. Imagine that ten different persons each had one of the following jobs. *Based on what you know about this country*, how would you rank these persons according to the way others would tend to look up at them? Put number one (1) by the person who would be most looked up to, number two (2) by the person who whould be second most looked up to *and so on*.

The Office Clerk	The Farmer
The Doctor	The Carpenter
The Coal Miner	The Electrical Engineer
The Member of Parliament	The Shop Assistant
The Policeman	The Businessman

31. Let us suppose that you were free to choose any job that you wished. What job *would you like* to have more than any other? Please describe the job carefully.

32. What kind of job do you think you are *most likely to get* when you start work?

33. What kind of things are likely to prevent you from having the job you would most like to have?

34. What do you think of the following sentence? 'Most of the people who get the best jobs in this country thoroughly deserve to do so.'
    1. I strongly agree with the above sentence.
    2. I agree with the above sentence.
    3. I have no opinion one way or the other.
    4. I disagree with the above sentence.
    5. I strongly disagree with the above sentence.
    6. Don't know what to think.

35. Could you give the reasons why you have chosen this answer?

36. Today many people work for the government. It is quite common for those who work for the government to be doing a similar job as those who work for private industry. Imagine that you had the chance of doing *exactly the same job, at exactly the same pay*, for either the government or a private industry. In such a case for whom would you choose to work?
    1. I would work for a private industry.
    2. I would work for the government.
    3. If the job were the same I would not mind for whom I worked.

37. Could those of you who have selected to work *either* for *the government or* for a *private industry* list the reasons for your choice?

38. Is you father at present working?   1. Yes
                                          2. No

39. If your father is *not* at present working could you please tell me the name of his *last* job. If you don't know the name of the job tell me all that you can about it.

40. If your father *is* at present working, does he work for himself or is he employed by someone else (in a company, industry, or on a farm, etc.)?

    1. He works for himself

    2. He works for someone else

41. If he *works for himself* could you tell me exactly what he does. If he has people working for him could you tell me approximately how many?

    1. My father's exact job is as follows:

    2. The number of people he has working for him is approximately:

42. If he *works for someone else* could you tell me exactly what job he is doing? If you are not sure of the exact job tell me all you can about it.

43. Does your mother work somewhere?

    1. Housewife only.

    2. Regular job, full time.

    3. Regular job, part time.

44. If she is at present working, full time or part time, could you tell me exactly what she does? If you don't know the exact job tell me all you can about it.

45. Although not working at present your mother may have worked in the past. If you know tell me the name of your mother's *last* job. If you don't know the exact job tell me all you can about it. *If in the previous question you have told me the name of your mother's present job there is no need to answer this question.*

Here again is a different set of questions.

46. Which political party does your father support?

    1. The Conservative party.

    2. The Labour party.

    3. The Liberal party

    4. He does not support any party.

    5. Don't know.

47. Which political party does your mother support?

    1. The Conservative party.

    2. The Labour party.

    3. The Liberal party.

4. She does not support any party.

5. Don't know.

48. How interested would you say your parents are in politics?
1. Very interested
2. Interested
3. Not very interested
4. Not interested

49. How interested would you say you are in politics?
1. Very interested
2. Interested
3. Not very interested
4. Not interested

50. Let us assume you were old enough to support a political party. Which of the political parties would you be most likely to support?
1. The Conservative party
2. The Labour party
3. The Liberal party
4. I would not support any party
5. Don't know

51. The following list contains different political positions. Which one would you yourself *like to be*?
1. A clerk at the town hall
2. Local councillor
3. Important civil servant in London
4. A Member of Parliament
5. None of the above
6. Don't know

52. The following list contains the same set of different political positions. Which one could a person like yourself *expect to have*?
1. A clerk at the town hall
2. Local councillor
3. Important civil servant in London
4. A Member of Parliament
5. None of the above
6. Don't know

53. What kind of things are likely to prevent you from obtaining the political position you would most like to have?

54. Here is a set of statements about our parliamentary system of government. These statements refer to our system in general and not to the way a particular party acts while in office.
Which of them *best represents* your own opinion?
    1. The British people have no say in how the country is governed
    2. Our system of government often seems to be out of touch with the people
    3. I have no opinion one way or the other
    4. Our system of government usually acts to suit the people
    5. Our system of government always represents the wishes of the people
    6. Don't know what to think

55. Could you give the reasons why you have chosen this answer?

56. People feel differently about Britain. Which of the following statements best sums up your own feelings?
    1. Britain is the finest country in the world
    2. On the whole it is a good country
    3. I have no opinion one way or the other
    4. There are many things I should like to see changed
    5. I will leave as soon as it is possible
    6. Don't know what to think

Here is the final set of questions:

57. It is often said that there are different social classes in this country. List the social classes you think exist in Britain.

58. To which of these social classes do you and your family belong?

59. To what social class would you *like to belong* once you have left school and set up a family of your own?

60. To what social class do you *expect to belong* once you have left school and set up a family of your own?

61. What kind of things are likely to prevent you from belonging to the social class you would most like to belong to?

62. Which of these statements best sums up your opinion of the relationship between classes in Britain?
    1. Class relations could not be worse than at present
    2. Steps should be taken to remove some of the class differences
    3. I have no opinion one way or the other
    4. Class relations are about right at present
    5. Class relations in this country are better than in any other country
    6. Don't know what to think

63. Could you give the reasons why you have chosen this answer?

64. *Based on what you know about this country* how would you rank the following items as being important in placing an individual in a particular social class? Put number one (1) by the item you think in most important, number two (2) by the item that you think is second most important *and so on.*
    His education
    His parents and family background
    The way he acts and treats others
    His job
    The way he speaks
    His money and wealth

65.* Do you think that the London area has as much to say in the governing of the country as other regions (for example the North of England)?
    1. The London area has less to say
    2. The London are has about the same to say
    3. The London area has more to say
    4. Don't know what to think

66.** If you were offered a job in Manchester, with better prospects than most of the jobs available in the London area, would you be prepared to go and live there?
    1. I would definitely go
    2. I would most likely go

* Depending on where the questionnaire was administered, 'the London area' and 'the North of England' were interchanged.
** Depending on where the questionnaire was administered, 'Manchester and 'the London area' were interchanged.

3. I am not sure what I would do
4. I would most likely stay
5. Under no circumstances would I leave

If there are any comments you would like to make on this questionnaire, please do so in the available space.

BIBLIOGRAPHY

Abrams, P., and Little, A., 'The Young Voter in British Politics', *British Journal of Sociology*, 16, 1965, 95–110.

Abrams, M., and Rose, R., *Must Labour Lose?* Harmondsworth, Penguin Books, 1960.

Almond, G. A., and Verba, S., *The Civic Culture*, Princeton, Princeton University Press, 1963.

Bene, E., 'Family Size and the Ability to Pass the Grammar School Entrance Examination', *Educational Review*, 10, 1957–58, 226–32.

— 'Some Differences between Middle Class and Working Class Grammar School Boys in their Attitudes towards Education', *British Journal of Sociology*, 10, 1959, 148–52.

Berelson, B., *et al.*, *Voting*, Chicago, Chicago University Press, 1954.

Bernstein, B., 'Social Class and Linguistic Development: A Theory of Social Learning', in Halsey, A. H. (ed.) *et al.*, *Education, Economy and Society*, New York, The Free Press 1961, 288–314.

Blair Hood, H., 'Occupational Preferences of Secondary Modern School-children', *Educational Review*, 4, 1951, 55–64.

Blondel, J., *Voters, Parties and Leaders*, Harmondsworth, Penguin Books, 1963.

Burdick, E., and Brodbeck, A. J. (eds.), *American Voting Behavior*, Glencoe, The Free Press, 1959.

Burt, C., 'Ability and Income', *The British Journal of Educational Psychology*, 13, 1943, 83–98.

Butler, D., and Rose, R., *The British General Election of 1959*, London, Macmillan, 1960.

— and Stokes, D., *Political Change in Britain*, London, Macmillan, 1969.

BIBLIOGRAPHY

Butler, R., *English Secondary School Adolescents: An Analysis of Political Discontent*, Unpublished M.A. thesis, the University of Sussex, 1969.

Campbell, A. *et al.*, *The Voter Decides*, Illinois, Row, Peteron, 1954.

— *The American Voter*, New York, Wiley, 1960.

— *Elections and the Political Order*, New York, Wiley, 1966.

Campbell, W. J., 'The Influence of the Home Environment on the Educational Progress of Selective Secondary School Children', *British Journal of Educational Psychology*, 22, 1952, 89–100.

Central Advisory Council for Education, *Early Leaving*, London, H.M.S.O., 1954.

Child, I., *Italian or American: Second Generation in Conflict*, New Haven, Yale University Press, 1943.

— 'Socialization', in G. Lindzey (ed.), *Handbook of Social Psychology*, Volume 2, Cambridge, Mass., Addison-Wesley, 1954, 655–92.

Chown, S. M., 'The Formation of Occupational Choice among Grammar School Pupils', *Occupational Psychology*, 32, 1958, 171–82.

Clarke, E. L., 'The Recruitment of the Nation's Leaders', *Sociological Review*, 28, 1936, 246–66.

Clements, R. V., *The Choice of Careers by School Children*, Manchester, Manchester University Press, 1958.

Collins, M., 'The Causes of Premature Leaving from the Grammar Schools, Part One', *British Journal of Educational Psychology*, 24, 1954, 129–42.

— 'The Causes of Premature Leaving from the Grammar Schools, Part Two', *British Journal of Educational Psychology*, 25, 1955, 23–5.

Conway, J., 'The Inheritance of Intelligence and its Social Implications', *British Journal of Social Psychology*, 11, 1958, 171–90.

Dahl, R., *A Preface to Democratic Theory*, Chicago, The University Press, 1956.

— *Who Governs?*, New Haven, Yale University Press, 1961.

Davies, J., 'The Family's Role in Political Socialization', *The Annals*, 361, 1965, 10–19.

Davis, R., *The Grammar School*, Harmondsworth, Pelican, 1967.

Dawson, R., and Prewitt, K., *Political Socialization*, Boston, Little Brown, 1969.

Dennis, J., 'Major Problems of Political Socialization Research', *Midwest Journal of Political Science*, 12, 1968, 85–114.

BIBLIOGRAPHY

Department of Education and Science, *The Organization of Secondary Schools* (Circular 10/65), London, H.M.S.O., 1965.

Douglas, J. W. B., *The Home and the School*, London, MacGibbon and Kee, 1964.

— *et al.*, *All Our Future*, London, Peter Davies, 1968.

Easton, D., and Dennis, J., 'The Child's Image of Government', *The Annals*, 361, 1965, 40–57.

— Dennis, J., 'The Child's Acquisition of Regime Norms: Political Efficacy', *American Political Science Review*, 61, 1967, 25–38.

— Dennis, J., *Children in the Political System*, New York, McGraw-Hill, 1969.

— and Hess, R., 'The Child's Political World', *Midwest Journal of Political Science*, 6, 1962, 229–46.

— and Hess, R., 'Youth and the Political System', in Lipset, S. M., and Lowenthal, L. (eds), *Cultural and Social Character*, New York, The Free Press, 1961, 226–51.

Eckstein, H., *A Theory of Stable Democracy*, Princeton, Centre of International Studies, 1961.

Elkin, R., *The Child and Society*, New York, Random House, 1960.

Erikson, E., *Childhood and Society*, New York, Norton, 1950.

Floud, J., 'Educational Opportunity and Social Mobility', *Year Book of Education*, 1950, 117–35.

— 'Education and Social Class in the Welfare State', in Judges, A. V. (ed.), *Looking Forward in Education*, London, Faber, 1955, 38–59.

— and Halsey, A. H., 'Education and Occupation: English Secondary Schools and the Supply of Labour', *Year Book of Education*, 1956, 519–32.

— and Halsey, A. H., 'Intelligence Tests, Social Class and Selection for Secondary School', *British Journal of Sociology*, 8, 1957, 33–39.

— and Halsey, A. H., 'The Sociology of Education', *Current Sociology*, 7, 1958, 165–93.

— *et al.*, *Social Class and Educational Opportunity*, London, Heinemann, 1956.

Ford, J., *Social Class and the Comprehensive School*, London, Routledge and Kegan Paul, 1969.

Ford, T. R., 'Social Factors Affecting Academic Performance: Further Evidence', *School Review*, 65, 1957, 415–22.

Froman, L. A., 'Personality and Political Socialization', *Journal of Politics*, 23, 1961, 341–52.

BIBLIOGRAPHY

Froman, L. A., 'Learning Political Attitudes', *Western Political Quarterly*, 15, 1962, 304–14.

Galler, E. H., 'Influence of Social Class on Children's Choice of Occupation', *Elementary School Journal*, 5, 1950–51, 439–45.

Glass, D. V., 'Education and Social Change in Modern Britain', in Halsey, A. H. (ed.), *Education, Economy and Society*, New York, The Free Press, 1961, 391–413.

— (ed.), *Social Mobility in Great Britain*, London, Routledge and Kegan Paul, 1954.

— and Hall, J. R., 'A Study of Inter-Generational Changes In Status' in Glass, D. V. (ed.), *Social Mobility in Great Britain*, London, Routledge and Kegan Paul, 177–217.

Goldthorpe, J. H., and Lockwood, D., 'Affluence and the British Class Structure', *Sociological Review* (New Series), 1, 1963, 133–163.

Gray, J. L. and Mohinsky, P., 'Ability and Opportunity in English Education' in Hogben L. (ed.), *Political Arithmetic*, London, Allen and Unwin, 1938, 334–76.

— and Mohinsky, P., 'Ability and Educational Opportunity in Relation to Parental Occupation', in Hogben, L. (ed.), *Political Arithmetic*, London, Allen and Unwin, 1938, 377–417.

Greenstein, F. I., *Children and Politics*, New Haven, Yale University Press, 1965.

— 'The Benevolent Leader: Children's Images of Political Authority', *American Political Science Review*, 54, 1960, 934–43.

— 'More on Children's Images of the President', *Public Opinion Quarterly*, 25, 1961, 648–54.

— 'Popular Images of the President', *American Journal of Psychiatry*, 122, 1965, 523–29.

— 'The Psychological Function of the American President for Citizens', in Cornwell, E. E. (ed.), *The American Presidency: Vital Center*, Chicago, Scott-Foresman, 1966, 30–6.

Haggard, E. H., 'Socialization, Personality and Academic Achievement in Gifted Children', *School Review*, 65, 1957, 388–414.

Hall, J. R., and Glass, D. V., 'Education and Social Mobility', in Glass, D. V. (ed.), *Social Mobility in Great Britain*, London, Routledge and Kegan Paul, 1954, 291–307.

Halsey, A. H., and Gardner, L., 'Selection for Secondary Education and Achievement in Four Grammar Schools', *British Journal of Sociology*, 4, 1953, 60–75.

168

BIBLIOGRAPHY

— et al., *Education, Economy and Society*, New York, The Free Press, 1961.

Hargreaves, D. H., *Social Relations in a Secondary School*, London, Routledge and Kegan Paul, 1967.

Havighurst, R. J., and David, A., 'Child Socialization and the School', *Review of Educational Research*, 13, 1943, 29–37.

Hess, R. D., 'The Socialization of Attitudes Toward Political Authority: Some Cross-National Comparisons', *International Social Science Journal*, 15, 1963, 542–59.

— and Easton, D., 'The Child's Changing Image of the President', *Public Opinion Quarterly*, 24, 1960, 632–44.

— and Torney, J., *The Development of Political Attitudes in Children*, Chicago, Aldine, 1967.

Himmelweit, H. T., et al., 'The Views of Adolescents on Some Aspects of the Social Class Structure', *British Journal of Sociology*, 3, 1952, 148–72.

Hoggart, R., *The Uses of Literacy*, Harmondsworth, Penguin Books, 1958.

Holly, D. N., 'Profiting from a Comprehensive Education: Class, Sex and Ability', *British Journal of Sociology*, 16, 1965, 502–11.

Hyman, H., *Political Socialization*, Glencoe, The Free Press, 1959.

Jackson, B., *Streaming: An Education System in Miniature*, London, Routledge, 1964.

— and Marsden, D., *Education and the Working Class*, London, Routledge and Kegan Paul, 1962.

Jahoda, G., 'Job Attitude and Job Choice Among Secondary Modern Leavers', *Occupational Psychology*, 26, 1952, 125–40.

— 'The Development of Children's Ideas about Country and Nationality, Part 1: The Conceptual Framework', *The British Journal of Educational Psychology*, 33, 1963, 47–60.

— 'The Development of Children's Ideas about Country and Nationality, Part II: National Symbols and Themes', *The British Journal of Educational Psychology*, 33, 1963, 143–53.

Jaros, D., et al., 'The Malevolent Leaders: Political Socialization in an American Subculture', *American Political Science Review*, 62, 1968, 564–75.

Jennings, M. Kent, 'Pre-Adult Orientations to Multiple Systems of Government', *Midwest Journal of Political Science*, 11, 1967, 291–317.

Jennings, M. Kent, and Niemi, R. G., 'The Transmission of Political Values from Parent to Child', *American Political Science Review*, 62, 1968, 169–84.

Jensen, A. R., 'How Much Can We Boost I.Q. and Scholastic Achievement', Harvard Educational Review, 39, 1969, 1–123.

Judges, A. V. (ed.), *Looking Forward in Education*, London, Faber, 1955.

Kenniston, K., *The Young Radicals*, New York, Harcourt, 1968.

Labour Party, *Signposts for the Sixties*, London, 1961.

Lacey, C., 'Some Sociological Concomitants of Academic Streaming in Grammar School', *British Journal of Sociology*, 17, 1966, 245–62.

Lane, R. E., *Political Life*, Chicago, The Free Press, 1959.

— *Political Ideology*, New York, Macmillan, 1962.

— 'Fathers and Sons: Foundation of Political Belief', *American Sociological Review*, 24, 1959, 502–11.

— and Sears, D. O., *Public Opinion*, New Jersey, Prentice Hall, 1964.

Langton, K., *Political Socialization*, New York, Oxford University Press, 1969.

Lazarsfeld, P., *et al.*, *The People's Choice*, New York, Columbia University Press, 1949.

Lenski, G., 'Status Crystallisation: A Non-Vertical Dimension of Social Status', *American Sociological Review*, 19, 1954, 405–13.

Levin, M. B., *The Alienated Voter*, New York, Holt, Rinehart and Winston, 1960.

Levine, R., 'Political Socialization and Cultural Change', in Geertz, C. (ed.), *Old Societies and New States*, Glencoe, The Free Press, 1963, 280–303.

Lindsay, K., *Social Progress and Educational Waste*, London, Routledge and Kegan Paul, 1926.

Lipset, S. M., *Political Man*, London, Heinemann, 1960.

Litt, E., 'Civic Education, Community Norms and Political Indoctrination', American Sociological Review, 28, 1963, 69–75.

Little, A., and Westergaard, J., 'The Trend of Class Differentials in Educational Opportunity', *British Journal of Sociology*, 15, 1964, 301–15.

Liversidge, W., 'Life Chances', *Sociological Review* (New Series), 10, 1962, 17–34.

Lunn, J. Barker, *Streaming in the Primary School*, Slough, Bucks., N.R.E.R., 1970.

BIBLIOGRAPHY

Maccoby, E., *et al.*, 'Youth and Political Change', *Public Opinion Quarterly*, 18, 1954, 23–39.

Martin, F. M., 'An Inquiry into Parents' Preferences in Secondary Education', in Glass D. V. (ed.), *Social Mobility in Great Britain*, London, Routledge and Kegan Paul, 1954, 160–174.

McKenzie, R. T., and Silver, A., *Angels in Marble*, London, Heinemann, 1968.

Merriam, C., *The Making of Citizens: A Comparative Study of Methods of Civic Training*, Chicago, The University Press, 1931.

Middleton, R., and Putney, S., 'Political Expression of Adolescent Rebellion', *American Journal of Sociology*, 68, 1962, 527–35.

Miller, W. G., *Values in the Comprehensive School*, London, Oliver Boyd, 1961.

Mitchell, W. G., *The American Polity*, New York, The Free Press, 1962.

Musgrove, F., *Youth and the Social Order*, London, Routledge and Kegan Paul, 1964.

— *Family, Education and Society*, London, Routledge, 1966.

Nordlinger, E., *The Working Class Tories*, Berkeley, University of California Press, 1968.

Parsons, T., 'The School Class as a Social System: Some of its Functions in American Society', in Halsey, A. H., *et al.*, *Education, Economy and Society*, New York, The Free Press, 1961, 447–8.

— and Bales, R., *Family Socialization and Interaction Process*, Glencoe, The Free Press, 1965.

Pedley, R., *The Comprehensive School*, Harmondsworth, Penguin Books, 1963.

Plato, *The Republic*, Oxford, Clarendon Press, 1951.

Prewitt, K., 'Political Socialization and Leadership Selection', *The Annals*, 361, 1965, 96–111.

Pye, L. W., *Politics, Personality and Nation Building: Burma's Search for Identity*, New Haven, Yale University Press, 1962.

Rees, A. N., and Smith, T., *Town Councillors: A Study of Barking*, London, Acton Trust Society, 1965.

Rose, R., *Students in Society*, Manchester, University of Manchester Union, 1963.

— *Politics in England*, London, Faber, 1965.

— *People in Politics*, London, Faber, 1970.

Rubinstein, D., and Simon, B., *The Evolution of the Comprehensive School, 1926–1966*, London, Routledge and Kegan Paul, 1969.

BIBLIOGRAPHY

Runciman, W. G., *Relative Deprivation and Social Justice*, London, Routledge and Kegan Paul, 1966.

Sigel, R. S., 'Image of a President: Some Insights into the Political Views of School Children', *American Political Science Review*, 62, 1968, 216–226.

— 'Image of the Presidency–Part II of an Exploration into Popular Views', *Midwest Journal of Political Science*, 40, 1966, 123–37.

Stephenson, R. M., 'Stratification, Education and Occupational Orientation', *British Journal of Sociology*, 9, 1958, 42–52.

Stevens, F., *The Living Tradition*, London, Hutchinson, 1960.

Stinchcombe, A., *Rebellion in a High School*, Chicago, Quadrangle Books, 1964.

Swift, D. F., *Social Class, Mobility-Ideology and the 11 Plus*, paper prepared for the Research Group, Sociology of Education, Sixth World Congress of Sociology, Evian, France, 1966.

Tawney, R. H., *Secondary Education for All*, London, Allen and Unwin, 1922.

Taylor, W., *The Secondary Modern School*, London, Faber, 1963.

— 'Secondary Modern Examinations and Social Mobility in England', *Journal of Sociology*, 34, 1960, 1–6.

Thompson, J. W., 'Genetics, Social Structure, Intelligence and Statistics', *British Journal of Sociology*, 11, 1960, 44–50.

Turner, R. H., 'Modes of Social Ascent through Education: Sponsored and Contest Mobility', in Halsey, A. H., *et al.*, *Education, Economy and Society*, New York, The Free Press, 1961, 121–39.

Verba, S., *The Comparative Study of Political Socialization*, paper delivered at the A.G.M. of the American Political Science Association, Chicago, 1964.

Wrong, D. H., 'The Oversocialized Conception of Man in Modern Sociology', *American Sociological Review*, 26, 1961, 183–93.

Young, M., *The Rise of the Meritocracy*, Harmondsworth, Penguin Books, 1961.

— *Innovation and Research in Education*, London, Routledge and Kegan Paul, 1965

— and Willmott, P., *Family and Kinship in East London*, London, Routledge and Kegan Paul, 1957.

INDEX

Subjects

INDEX

Authors

INDEX

Monks, T. G., 18, 25
Musgrove, F., 124

Parkes, A. S., 15
Parsons, T., 41–2
Partridge, J., 32–3, 63–4
Plato, 27
Polk, K., 35

Rees, A. M., 82–3
Robbins Report, 14
Rose, R., 99, 119, 142
Ross, J. M., 24

Simpson, H. R., 24
Smith, T., 82–3
Spens Report, 18
Stenhouse, L., 28–9, 34
Stevens, F., 71, 119
Stinchcombe, A. L., 43

Stokes, D., 95

Tawney, R. H., 13, 18
Taylor, W., 17, 32
The Times, 25, 147–9, 152
Torney, J. V., 28
Townsend, P., 22, 23
Troday, J. M., 15
Turner, R. H., 77

Verba, S., 57, 100, 123
Vernon, P. E., 15, 16, 17, 24

Walker, P. Gordon, 20
Westley, W. A., 35
Wilkinson, R., 28, 36–7
Willmott, P., 98
Wilson, H., 18

Young, M., 23, 43, 49, 62, 98